An Indispens

Dangerou

An Indispensible Guide to

Dangerous English!

for Language Learners and Others

by

Elizabeth Claire

Pictures by

eluki bes shahar

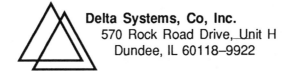

Delta Systems, Co, Inc.
570 Rock Road Drive, Unit H
Dundee, IL 60118–9922

ISBN 0–937354–47–3

 Delta Systems, Co, Inc.
570 Rock Road Drive, Unit H
Dundee, IL 60118–9922

Printed in the U.S.A.

Contents

Introduction

An Indispensible Guide to Dangerous English! was originally published as *A Foreign Student's Guide to Dangerous English!* The guide has been revised and updated, and contains these new features:

- hundreds of new words

- more pictures to clarify meanings

- dangerous nonverbal communication in gestures, touching and personal distance

- dangerous ethnic terms and insults

- common reproductive or urogenital medical conditions and doctors' procedures

- explanations of movie ratings

- explanations of religious taboo words and their euphemisms

- new format for dangerous synonyms

Acknowledgments

I would like to gratefully acknowledge the encouragement, assistance and the scholarship of the world's foremost authority on dangerous words in any language, Dr. Reinhold Aman, editor of *Maledicta, The International Journal of Verbal Aggression*.

There are many other friends and colleagues to whom I owe a debt of gratitude for their reports on current use of the words included in this book. They served as my ears into places I do not go, and told me the words that wouldn't be spoken in my presence even if I had gone. As I promised them, their contributions shall remain anonymous, but definitely not unappreciated.

Thanks to Janet Cuccinelli for her courageous and medically expert copyediting, and to Terri Lehmann for research, office support, and all-around gofering. Thanks to David Corona, of David Corona Design, for the special care he took with the design, typesetting, paging and all-around expediting of the production.

I'd also like to thank Dick Patchin, of Delta Systems for his market vision for the new edition of the book, making it available at a modest cost to the many new speakers of English who need it.

About the Author

Believe it or not, Elizabeth Claire is a mild-mannered grandmother from New Jersey. She graduated magna cum laude from the City College of New York, was elected into Phi Beta Kappa, and received the Downer Medal of Excellence for Hispanic Studies. She received the her Master's Degree in TESOL from New York University under an Experienced Teacher Fellowship Program. She has taught English as a Second Language for twenty years to students of all ages, and wrote the original edition of *Dangerous English* because she was too embarrassed to explain terms she knew her students wanted and needed. When, in 1980, no publishing company was willing to take the risk of publishing this guide, she borrowed money from her even milder-mannered mother to produce and market the work that has since become a classic in the field. Ms. Claire is currently a materials writer, teacher trainer and ESL consultant.

Her other books are all completely safe for classroom use! They are:

Three Little Words: A, An, and The *(A Foreign Student's Guide to English Articles)*

What's So Funny? *(A Foreign Student's Guide to American Humor)*

The ESL Teacher's Activities Kit

The ESL Teacher's Holiday Activities Kit

The ESL Wonder Workbooks
- #1 This Is Me
- #2 All Around Me

HI! ESL for Children

HI! Teacher's Guide

Just a Minute! An Oral Language–Learning Game

To the Teacher

You may think twice before using *An Indispensible Guide to Dangerous English* in your classroom. After all, it *is* dangerous. These interesting and useful words are highly charged with social taboos. But one thing is for sure: most of your students will learn the concepts and expressions in this book with less effort and more involvement than any other subject matter in English!

Sentences are kept short, new words are explained, and grammatical patterns are fairly simple. An adult student at the intermediate level of ESL can handle the material with some instruction and discussion. An advanced student may be able to progress on his or her own.

Here are some ideas that have worked for other instructors of adult ESL students. Choose among these options:

A. Separate your class into two groups: Teach the group that is the same sex as you are, and ask a colleague or "guest lecturer"of the opposite sex to teach the other group. Be very clear with your students in advance about the content you are going to be covering so that students who don't want to participate can have an alternative assignment.

B. Even if you are comfortable talking about these terms to a mixed audience, your students may not be. Announce, "Next week we will talk about sexual and bathroom terms. If any of you think you will find this embarrassing or offensive, see me after class today for an alternative assignment for you. You won't have to come to class. If you complete this other assignment, you won't be marked absent." Use one or two class periods to get the students started with the basics and have them continue on their own. (The teachers who have used this technique report that no one has ever taken the option to do an alternative assignment.)

C. Organize a new class for the specific purpose of learning slang and vulgar English. There is enough material for discussion and vocabulary learning for a five-week course that meets two hours a week. Supplement it with some "R" movies of the "tough cop" variety as outside assignments.

D. Keep a few copies of *Dangerous English* on a reference shelf. Make students aware of the book's existence and the nature of its contents, and allow them to borrow a copy and study it in private.

E. Order copies for your students' own use, or have them order their own. You may photocopy the order blank at the end of the book.

If you have chosen to use *Dangerous English* as a text for classroom instruction, here are some further suggestions:

Announce that they will be using a book called *Dangerous English*. What do they think the title means? What would Dangerous Japanese, or Dangerous Spanish mean to them? What kinds of words would they put in a book of Dangerous ___ of their own language?

Read the overview, "What is 'Dangerous English'?" Conduct a discussion to find out what their concerns are in this area of language. For example, some students may be more concerned about learning correct anatomical terms and their correct pronunciation and avoiding the unintended use of vulgar language. Others may want to know what the guys in the dorms are talking about, and how to fit in. Others will be most interested in the cultural insights that a study of expressions will reveal.

Let your students know your feelings about the words. After all, words are only sounds, but they can generate powerful visceral reactions. Confess your embarrassment if you feel it. Or your general amusement at the words if that's what you feel. Let them know that, in any case, people vary in their reactions, and you expect them to have varied reactions. The difference is that Americans have been conditioned to react in certain ways to the sounds of these dangerous terms, but to your students, it will just be new sounds. The danger lies in the lack of a conditioned awareness of the reactions different groups of Americans will have when they hear these words spoken.

To the new speaker of English, *pansy, nigger, prick, and pussy* don't sound any worse than *daisy, nickel, prince, and bossy.* Convey your own feelings, but also convey the feelings others will have to the words. Caution them to err on the side of prudery until they have become completely familiar with their social environment and can predict people's reactions.

Elicit their stories of embarrassing moments with English.

Read "The Social Classes of English Words." Ask if there are such classes of words in their own language. Are there additional categories? Informally quiz them to be sure they are absolutely clear about the different levels and situations to which the words apply. Ask if they can take a sexual or bathroom term in their own language and write the synonyms for it, grouping the words into the six categories. Do they notice a difference in feeling when they say a formal word, a euphemism, and a slang equivalent for the same body part in their own language?

Go over the pronunciation guide on the inside front cover, to be sure they can use it effectively.

Proceed with each section by having students preread the selection before class, or silently during class. Prepare questions for discussion relating the new concepts to their own language, or just allow for questions, answers, and anecdotes. Provide a model for pronunciation and intonation. If there are words you'd rather not say, have a colleague make a cassette recording that you can play in class. Focus on the interest areas that meet your students' needs.

If you need encouragement to use
An Indispensible Guide to Dangerous English
*with your adult students, here's what other professionals have
said about the first edition:*

". . . Our ESL students hear taboo words all the time. But they do not always notice *who* uses *which* words, *when, how,* and under *what circumstances.* Of course, we do not want to teach our students to use dangerous words indiscriminately, or as much as they may hear peers using them . . . I am *not* advocating a wholesale adoption of lessons based on taboo words . . . But if we (ESL teachers) do not tell them the limits of general acceptability, it is all too probable that no one else will . . . Too often, learners find out dangerous words by making an embarrasing and unintentional *double entendre;* students appreciate knowing some of the more obvious pitfall in advance . . . . There is a need for adressing this area of language because our students need it: they have medical or sexual problems . . . that they have to talk about with counselors and doctors; they go to movies, read novels, . . . hear and sometimes use language we don't use in the classroom; . . . they want to understand jokes — in short, become competent users of the language.

. . . *A Foreign Student's Guide to Dangerous English* can fulfill a real need for learners of English as a second language (and not few native speakers as well!) . . . basically clear and well done."

— **Lisa Werner,** Universite de Montreal, in the *TESOL Newsletter,*
June, 1982.

"The definitions . . . are neither prudish nor suggestive; the syntax and vocabulary used are simple enough to be within the range of a low-intermediate student . . . Is this a book that you should tell your adult students about so that they can order it if they're interested? Yes, indeed. The book will provide them with the American English words for acts and functions which they are already well aware of . . . The book answers a real need for adult students of English as a second language living in the U.S. and would be of interest and use to many foreign visitors. I suspect that any campus bookstore that stocks it will find they have a best-seller on their hands."

— **Jean McConochie,** Pace University, in the NYTESOL *IDIOM,*
May, 1981.

"... *A Foreign Student's Guide to Dangerous English* has impressed me greatly. This kind of knowledge is really important for the students of English in Japan. The work is an excellent one."

— **Professor Masayoshi Yamada,** Chairman, Department of English, Faculty of Education, Shimane University, Japan

"... an idea whose time is definitely here, ... intelligently written and illustrated."

— **The Los Angeles Herald Examiner.** Oct. 21, 1984.

"I commend you on your outstanding work in an area of language learning that most educators prefer to simply avoid."

— **Richard Seltzer,** University of Southern California

" Though containing rather 'delicate' material, the book is a most valuable resource guide for the adult professional non-native English speaker who hopes to learn to be at ease in casual American conversational groups. I congratulate you on your efforts."

— **James Hawkins,** Past President, TEXTESOL–III

What Is "Dangerous English"?

In every language, there are "dangerous" words. These are words that may be embarrassing for the speaker to say, or cause the listener to feel insulted, to become angry, or to judge the speaker in a negative way.

In English, most of these dangerous words refer to sexual parts of our bodies, sexual activities, and bathroom functions. Yet these words are among the most necessary, useful, and interesting words in our language.

Other words may be dangerous because they are forbidden by Christian or Jewish religious teachings.

Some words for racial or national groups are so dangerous they have caused violence and even murder.

You may hear words in movies, in the street, in the dormitory, in bars, or at parties that you should never use in class or in a business office. If you have children who learn these words from their friends, you need to be sure they don't say them in school.

If you came to this country as an adult, you have found that it is very difficult to learn about these words. Teachers do not use dangerous words in English classes; textbooks and bilingual dictionaries do not explain them; it is embarrassing, or even dangerous, to ask your neighbors about them.

The best way to learn about them is to have a very good American friend.

But what if you don't have such a friend?

Then this book was written for you. *An Indispensible Guide to Dangerous English* will be *your* good American friend. It will save you from many embarrassing situations and help you understand a very interesting part of American culture. Whether you want to learn to use this colorful language, or learn to avoid it, you need this book. We hope you enjoy it!

In this book, you will learn:

- the correct, scientific words for the sexual parts of your body and for sexual and bathroom activities. You will also learn the *most polite* terms to express these ideas.

- the words you need when you go to the doctor's office for male or female problems.

- the slang, vulgar, and children's words for body parts, sex and bathroom activities.

- other ways that vulgar terms are used in English, in hundreds of expressions that have nothing to do with sex or the bathroom.

- common words that have dangerous "double meanings."

- how to avoid pronunciation problems that may cause you embarrassment.

- about English words that look or sound similar to common words in *your* language, but have sexual or vulgar meanings in English.

- which religious words are dangerous in some situations.

- words for national and racial groups of people that are polite, and which terms are so dangerous they can cause violence!

- dangerous *nonverbal* English.

There are words in this book that you may never want to use. Nevertheless, it is natural to be curious about them. With *An Indispensible Guide to Dangerous English*, you will begin to understand an important aspect of American language and culture.

The Social Classes of English Words

There are two steps to learning about "dangerous" English. The first step is to know the meanings of the terms. Then you must know which words you can safely use in different social situations. To help you, we will use the following labels:

formal	*children's words*
general use	*slang*
euphemism	*vulgar*

1. **Formal** words are the "highest" words. Doctors, anatomy books, and biology textbooks use *formal* words. Use *formal* words whenever you want to be clear and exact. Both men andwomen use *formal* words. Children and people without a college education may not know the meaning of some *formal* words.

2. **General use** words are the best-known and most commonly used by American men and women. They are clear in their meanings. A word may be both *formal* and in *general use*. You may substitute a *general use* word in formal situations when you do not know the *formal* word. Many people are embarrassed to use *formal* or *general use* words. The meanings of these words are too clear. We prefer to be less clear when we talk about sex-related topics in public speeches or in polite conversation with someone we don't know very well.

3. **Euphemism** (pronounced yū´ fŭ mĭ z'm). A *euphemism* is a "polite" word that you may substitute for a *formal* or *general use* word. A *euphemism* is *less* clear and exact, but the meaning is understood. Euphemisms are commonly used in conversation with people you don't know very well, with

older people, or in mixed groups of both men and women. *Euphemisms are the safest words for the foreign student to use at first.*

Personal euphemisms may not be understood by the general public. A family or friends may invent terms to use when they are having a conversation in a public place. They do not wish other people to know that they are talking about sexual or bathroom matters.

Formal words, general use words, and most euphemisms are standard English and can be found in dictionaries. Children's words, slang, and vulgar words are not standard English. They exist mostly in spoken language; many cannot be found in standard dictionaries with their dangerous meanings explained.

4. *Children's words*. Many parents use special words with children that will be easy for them to pronounce while they are learning to talk. Later, special euphemisms may be used with children. Occasionally, adults may use *children's words* or "baby talk" to be funny.

5. *Slang* is used in social situations where a person feels comfortable with friends or associates. *Slang* adds humor, interest, and intimacy to the conversation. *Slang* words are often new words in the language, or old words that now have a new meaning. If the word becomes popular and people use it for many years, it may eventually be considered a *general use* word.

Slang may show an affectionate feeling or may be funny. Some *slang* terms are derogatory. (dē rŏ′gŭ tor′ ē)

Derogatory words show that the speaker intends to show superiority or contempt towards the object, act, or person he is talking about.

Offensive words are words that make a listener angry. Men often use slang and vulgar terms when they are talking about women's bodies. Many women find these terms *offensive*. Some slang terms for races and nationalities can be extremely *offensive* to listeners.

6. *Vulgar* words are the "lowest" social class of words. They are the "words of the common, uneducated people." Some people consider *all* vulgar terms for body parts and acts *offensive*.

Careful speakers *never* use *vulgar* words in formal situations, in the classroom, in the office, and in written work. Don't use *vulgar* words when speaking to teachers, superiors, older people, children, people you don't know very well, and mixed groups containing both men and women.

Vulgar words for sex and bathroom topics are sometimes called "dirty words," "four-letter words," "profanity," or "obscene language." To use vulgar language is called "swearing"or "cursing."

A person who uses vulgar language in the *wrong social situation* may be considered uneducated, immature, lower class, or immoral. On the other hand, a person who is easily offended by vulgar language may be considered a *prude*. (An overly fussy, moral, clean, old-fashioned person.)

Vulgar sex and toilet words are contained in many other expressions that have nothing to do with their original meaning. They are used to express anger, to show membership in a group, and to add humor and spice to speech.

Vulgar language is often used in all-male groups such as work teams or sports teams, men's college dormitories, the army, bars, and street gangs. Men of every social class from street cleaner to banker, and even a President of the United States, might use these words. In some settings, men use them in every sentence.

Years ago, polite men would never swear when a woman or a child was present. "Watch your language, there are ladies present" was a reminder. Today, women may not be surprised or offended to hear vulgar language at parties, and even at work. Many women also use vulgar language. However, they use fewer vulgar words and use them less frequently. Men expect vulgar language from men, and admire them for it. But they do not admire women for using vulgar language.

Teenagers may use vulgar language in order to be accepted by their group. Using forbidden words is a way of showing they are "growing up." They enjoy writing vulgar expressions on bathroom walls or buildings.

People with very little education may use vulgar terms because they do not know more formal words for their body parts and functions.

Some very *well*-educated people may prefer to use vulgar terms for the natural functions of the body. They feel that the formal words and euphemisms are *prudish*. They feel that the vulgar words are more honest and direct and express their feelings more accurately.

Lovers may often use vulgar words in the bedroom in their "love talk." These words seem more natural to some people than the scientifically correct or formal terms. They may also be more sexually exciting.

We don't know why, but vulgar language releases tension. Even people who don't usually swear may swear when they make a mistake, get upset, or hurt themselves. Anger brings out vulgar language, too. In a war of words, vulgar words are the weapons.

"Safe" and "Dangerous" Words for a Necessary Daily Function

The following words all refer to the same action and its product. But each word is correct only in its own special situation.

verb forms: Defecate, have a bowl movement, use the bathroom, make ka ka, make number two, go, take a shit.

noun forms: feces, stool, bowel movement, dirt, droppings, b.m., turds, shit.

1. **Formal:** *(Doctor to patient)*

   "We have to check a sample of your *stool*. When you *defecate,* use this special case to obtain a small *stool* sample. Bring it to the laboratory for testing."

   Formal: *(Restaurant inspector's written report)*

   "We found mouse *feces* on the shelves in the kitchen."

"Please bring a stool sample to the laboratory for testing."

2. **General Use:** *(A mother to another mother)*

"The baby hasn't *had a bowel movement* in two days. I wonder if I should give him a laxative? His *b.m.'s* have been very hard and dry."

3. **Euphemism:** *(Guest to host at a party)*

"May I *use your bathroom?*"

Euphemism: *(Woman to companion in the street)*

"Watch out! Don't step in the dog *dirt*."

4. **Children's words:** *(Three-year-old child)*

   "Mommy, I have to *make ka ka*."

   Children's words: *(Older child)*

   "Guess what? The dog *did number two* in the living room."

5. **Slang:** *(Any member of the family)*

   "Can we stop at a gas station soon? I have to *go!*"

   Slang: *(Friend to friend)*

   "Watch out! Don't step in the dog *turds!*"

6. **Vulgar:** *(In a college dormitory)*

   "Excuse me, I have to go *take a shit!*"

"Dangerous English" Goes to the Movies

There is a system for rating American movies. The ratings do not say how good the movies are. They only tell the level of sex, nudity, violence, and vulgar language that are included. (Nudity= men and women without clothes on. Violence = fighting, hurting, killing, blood).

"G"

"G" movies are for general audiences, including young children. There are no nude (unclothed) scenes, few scenes of violence, and no vulgar language.

"PG"

"PG"movies suggest that Parental Guidance is needed, and the movie is not good for young children. A "PG" movie may contain brief (short) sex scenes. The actors may be nude from the waist up for a brief time. Or a "PG" movie may contain some upsetting violence and vulgar language.

"R"

"R" movies are Restricted. That means that children under 18 years of age must be accompanied by an adult. "R" movies may contain a lot of nudity and sex, or a lot of violence, or both sex *and* violence. There may be a lot of vulgar language.

"X"

"X" movies are for adults 18 and older only. "X" movies are generally *pornographic*, with not much story at all. They are made for the purpose of sexual excitement. There are many detailed sex scenes, with possible perversions, nude bodies, and vulgar language.

• • •

Movies on major television networks today may be the "PG" type, with some sex and violence and vulgar language. Some "R" movies are shown late at night. Cable TV brings "R" and "X" movies to audiences at any time of day.

Only a few years ago, vulgar language was censored (cut out) on television. Each year, more vulgar words are becoming accepted on TV. This is upsetting to people who don't want to hear these words or who want to protect children from hearing them.

Before 1960, books with vulgar sexual language were not allowed in this country. Since then, writers have been free to write the words that show how their characters would speak in real life.

Safe Words for Dangerous Clothing

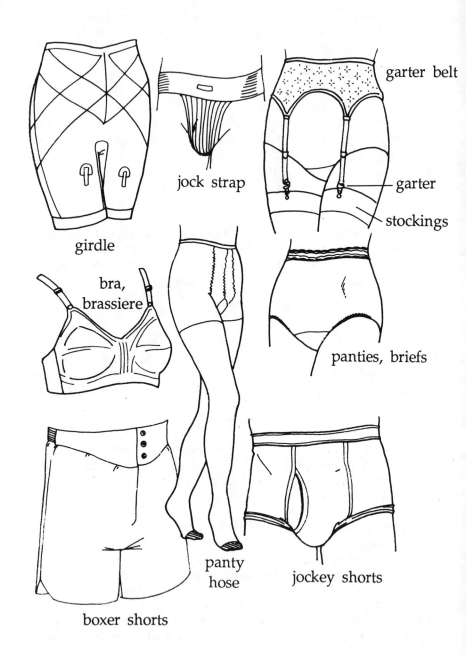

girdle

jock strap

garter belt

garter

stockings

bra, brassiere

panties, briefs

boxer shorts

panty hose

jockey shorts

Dangerous Words with Double Meanings

Many ordinary words have more than one meaning. You can easily learn the general meanings that are used in daily conversation. They will be taught in your classes and can be found in your textbooks and dictionaries.

But your teacher and your textbook may not teach you the slang or vulgar sexual and bathroom meanings of *those same words.* These meanings are well known to Americans, but bilingual dictionaries will not translate these dangerous double meanings into your language.

As a result, you may say something that is innocent to you but makes other people laugh. And they may never tell you why!

For example, the word *ball* has several general meanings.

ball   1. noun.   A round rubber toy. "The child is playing with a *ball.*" 2. Any sphere. "The sun is a *ball* of fire." 3. A game. "Let's play *ball.*" 4. A social party where people dress formally and dance to the music of an orchestra. "The president attended a *ball* in his honor." 5. In the game of baseball, a pitch that is not directly over the home plate. "*Ball* four!" shouted the umpire.

You may also know some of the slang uses. If you hear someone say, "I had a *ball* last night." you know that he means he had a very good time at some party or event.

But the dictionary and the classroom may not help you learn the sexual meanings of ball, even though every American adult knows them. And if you learn these words in the street you may never know the complete meaning or exactly when the words may be used.

ball 6. noun. vulgar. Testicle. "He scratched his *balls.*"
7. verb. vulgar. To have sexual intercourse with. "They *balled* all night."

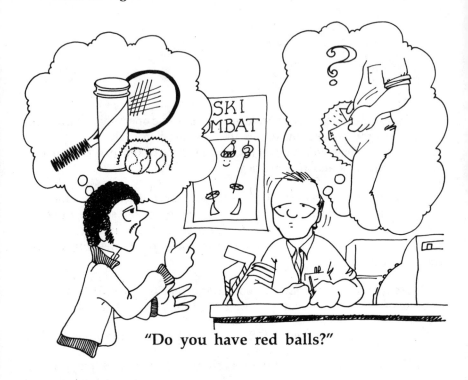

"Do you have red balls?"

In addition, there are several well-known expressions that contain the word *ball.*

to have balls verb phrase. vulgar. To have great masculine courage. "V. certainly *has balls* to argue with the boss."

it takes balls verb phrase. vulgar. A job or act that requires a person to have great courage. "*It takes balls* to be a race car driver."

to have someone by the balls   verb phrase. vulgar.
To be in a position capable of hurting someone (as though
you were holding his testicles). This may be physically,
financially, or legally. "I can't quit my job. The boss *has me
by the balls*. If I quit, he'll make me pay back the money he
lent to me immediately, and I can't afford to."

to bust one's balls   verb phrase. vulgar.   1. To work
very hard to complete a difficult job or to attain a goal. "L.
really *busted his balls* to finish the report on time."

to bust someone's balls   verb phrase. vulgar.   1. To
make a man lose power or self-esteem as a male. "K. enjoys
busting men's balls. She has a special way of making a man
feel inadequate and foolish. 2. To tease, man to man. "The
guys were *busting my balls* about my relationship with the
boss."

ball buster   noun. vulgar.   1. A difficult test or job.
"Professor J.'s test was a real *ball buster*; nobody was able to
answer all the questions." 2. A woman who makes a man
feel unmasculine. "Don't try to get friendly with T.; she's a
real *ball buster*. She'll make you feel like a three-year-old
child with her comments and insults."

oh balls!   vulgar.   An expression of disappointment or
annoyance. "*Oh, balls!* I can't find my new gloves."

How *Safe* Is *Your* English?
Test Yourself

Each of these ten words has a dangerous double meaning. You probably know the acceptable meanings, since the words are very common. How many of the sexual or bathroom meanings of these words do you know? Write the letter of your answer next to the word. Then check your answers on the next page.

1. bang _____   A. homosexual

2. bone _____   B. oral-genital sex

3. drawers _____   C. have sexual relations

4. eat _____   D. underpants

5. fairy _____   E. penis

6. number one _____   F. vagina

7. can _____   G. feces

8. come _____   H. have an orgasm

9. stool _____   I. urine

10. box _____   J. buttocks

Answers

1.	C	6.	I
2.	E	7.	J
3.	D	8.	H
4.	B	9.	G
5.	A	10.	F

How many did you get right? _____

1. **bang** (bang) 1. noun. general use. A loud noise, like the sound of a gun. "The door closed with a *bang*." 2. noun. slang. A thrill or special pleasure. "I get a *bang* out of watching little kids play baseball." 3. verb. vulgar. Have sexual intercourse with. Usually the subject is male, object female. "I'd really like to *bang* her," he said to his friend.

2. **bone** (bōn) 1. noun. general use. Part of a skeleton. "Your body has 206 *bones*." "The dog ate a *bone*." 2. verb. general use. To take the bones out of something. "The butcher will *bone* the fish for you." 3. verb. slang. *bone up*. To study for a test. "I can't go to the movies with you; I have to *bone up* for the history exam tomorrow." 4. noun. vulgar. The penis, especially when it is erect.

3. **drawers** (drorz) 1. noun, plural. general use. Parts of a desk, dresser, or other furniture. "His desk has three *drawers.*" 2. noun, plural. general use. Underpants. "Macy's is having a sale. I think I'll buy some new *drawers.*"

"I can't find the letter from XYZ Company. May I look in your drawers?"

4. **eat** 1. verb. general use. Chew and swallow food. "We *eat* three meals a day." 2. verb. vulgar. Perform cunnilingus or fellatio. (Lick or suck a partner's sex organs.)

5. **fairy** (fār´ ē) 1. noun. general use. A very small, imaginary, magical person, usually with wings. "The children love stories about *fairies.*" 2. noun. slang. A male homosexual. (This is a derogatory expression.)

6. **number one** 1. adjective. general use. The best, the most important. "Mr. J. is the *number one* man in that company. 2. noun. children's euphemism. Urine. "I have to make *number one.*"

7. **can** 1. noun. general use.   A round metal container. "Mother opened a *can* of tuna fish." 2. verb. general use. Be able. "John *can* speak four languages." 3. verb. general use.   To put something into cans or jars, such as food. "Rose *canned* four quarts of tomatoes from her garden." 4. noun. slang. The bathroom. The toilet. "Where's Joe?" "He's in the *can*." 5. noun. slang.   The buttocks. "I don't like to wear tight slacks because I have a big *can*."

8. **come** 1. verb. general use.   Arrive. "What time will you *come* to my house?" 2. To be packed in a certain kind of container. "Juice *comes* in pints and quarts." 3. To be available in a certain size, color, or style. "This blouse *comes* in red, green, and brown." (You may choose one of the colors.) 4. verb. vulgar.   Ejaculate. Have an orgasm. "'Did you *come*?' he asked. 'No, I didn't have time. You *came* too fast,' she answered."

9. **stool** (stūl) 1. noun. general use.   A chair without a back or arms. "The customers sat on the bar *stools*." 2. noun. formal. medical.   Feces, a bowel movement. "The doctor asked the patient to bring in a sample of his *stool*."

10. **box** 1. noun. general use.   A container: something you can put things in. "The child put his toys into a *box*." 2. verb. general use.   To put into a box. "The clerk *boxed* and wrapped the gift." 3. verb. general use.   To fight with one's fists, as in the sport of boxing. 4. noun. vulgar.   A woman's vagina.

More Dangerous Doubles

Here are some more of those dangerous words with double meanings. You will find the sexual or bathroom-related meanings in the synonyms section or the definitions section of this book.

adult	fly	nuts
affair	friend	organ
bag	fruit	overcoat
basket	gas	period
beat	gay	pet
beaver	go	Peter
behind	go down	piece
blow	hammer	piles
bottom	hard	private
briefs	head	put out
buns	hole	queer
brush	hot	relations
bush	hung	rocks
can	John	rubber
cheap	jugs	runs
cheat	knob	safety
cherry	knocker	satisfy
clap	lay	screw
come	loose	sixty-nine
crabs	lungs	swing
crack	madame	tail
cream	make	thing
Dick	meat	tool
dirty	member	trick
do	moon	turn on
drag	neck	withdraw
finger	number two	

Dangerous Synonyms and Related Words

In this section, you will learn many different words for each intimate part and function of the human body. Although the words refer to the same thing, they may not be substituted for each other. You will learn more about each word and how it is used in the Definitions section.

The Human Body

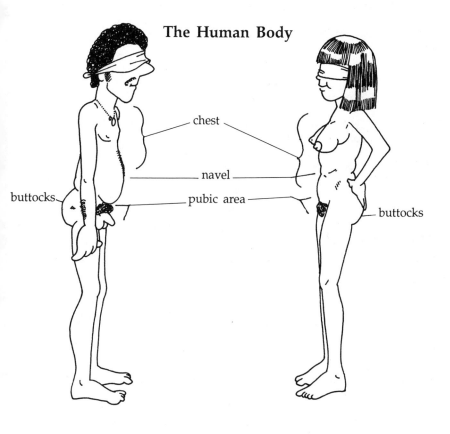

buttocks

chest

navel

pubic area

buttocks

A. The Human Body: Male or Female

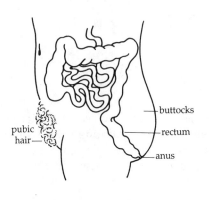

pubic hair — buttocks — rectum — anus

Formal pubic area, genitalia, groin, urogenitals

General Use sex organs

Euphemism crotch, down there, private parts, privates, loins, natural parts, secret parts

Slang see slang for male/ female

Vulgar see vulgar for male/ female

• • •

Formal buttocks, gluteus maximus

General Use buttocks

Euphemism behind, bottom, derriere, duff, posterior, rear end, seat, stern

Children's Words tush, tushie, tokus

Slang buns, butt, caboose, can, duster, fundament, hams, hind end, lower cheeks, moon, tail

Vulgar ass

• • •

Formal pubic hair

Slang beard, brush, bush (female), crab ladder, fur, garden, grass, lawn, moustache, rug, short hairs, wig, wool, fuzz

• • •

Formal rectum

General Use rectum, bowel, lower bowel

• • •

Formal buttocks, gluteus maximus

Slang rim, back door, brown eye, blind eye, poop chute

Vulgar ass hole, culo, shit hole

B. The Human Body: Male

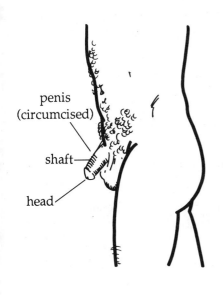

penis
(circumcised)

shaft

head

Formal penis, male organ

General Use penis

Euphemism apparatus, male member, member, "it," you-know-what

Children's Words thing, pee pee, peter, twinkie

Slang banana, bald-headed hermit, baloney, bird, carrot, cucumber, one-eyed worm, pickle, pipe, short arm, sugar stick, thing

Vulgar bone, bicho, cock, dick, dipstick, doodle, dork, dingus, hammer, horn, knob, joint, joystick, meat, pecker, peter, pork, prick, putz, schlong, tool, whang, wick

• • •

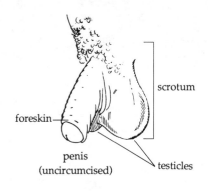

Formal testicles, testes, male gonads

General Use testicles

Euphemism delicate parts of the anatomy

Children's Words ballies

Slang apples, cohones, family jewels, equipment, rocky mountain oysters

Vulgar balls, knockers, nuts, rocks, stones

• • •

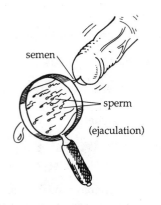

Formal semen, seminal fluid, spermatozoa

General Use semen, sperm

Euphemism seed

Slang love juice

Vulgar come, cream, jism

C. The Human Body: Female

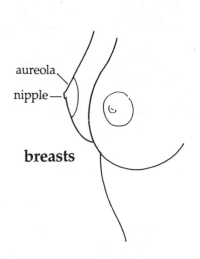

Formal breasts, mammary glands

General Use breasts

Euphemism chest, bust, bosom, front

Children's Words bubbies, titties

Slang apples, balloons, beauts, big brown eyes, coconuts, headlights, hemispheres, jugs, lungs, melons, Milky Way, pair, peaches, tonsils, watermelons

Vulgar boobs, boobies, knockers, milkers, teats, tits

• • •

Formal uterus

General Use uterus, womb

Euphemism stomach

Children's Words tummy, belly

Slang oven, pot

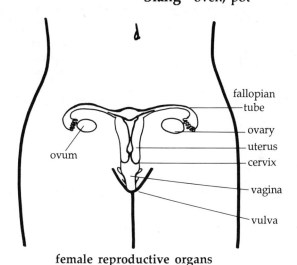

female reproductive organs

• • •

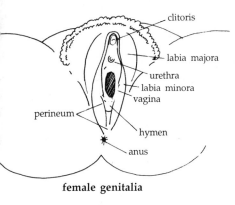

female genitalia

Formal vagina, birth canal, vulva, labia majora, labia minora

General Use vagina, birth canal

Euphemism down there, private parts

Vulgar ass, bearded clam, beaver, box, crack cunt, futz, hair pie, hole, manhole, meat, muff, piece, pussy, slit, snatch, twat

• • •

D. In the Bathroom

lid

flush
handle

toilet seat

tank

toilet
bowl

Formal   sanitary facilities

General Use   bathroom (in one's home), toilet

Euphemism   (in public places) comfort station, ladies' (mens') room, lavatory, lounge, powder room, restroom, washroom

Children's Words   potty, girls' room, boys' room

Slang   altar, can, the facilities, head, john, library, plumbing, smallest room, throne, throne room, used-beer department

Vulgar   crapper, shithouse, shitter

• • •

feces

Formal   feces, fecal matter, excrement, stool

General Use   bowel movement

Euphemism   b.m, waste material, dirt (dogs' or cats')

Children's Words   ah ah, doodoo, doody, ka ka, number two, poop, poopoo, poozie

Slang   crap, turds

Vulgar   shit, sinkers and floaters

• • •

defecate

Formal defecate, move one's bowels, have a bowel movement

General Use have a bowel movement

Euphemism go to the bathroom, go, make

Children's Words go, make, or do: ah ah, doodoo, doody, ka ka, number two, poop, poopoo, poozie

Slang use the facilities, see a man about a horse

Vulgar crap, dump, dump a load, pinch a loaf, shit, take a crap, take a dump, take a shit

• • •

Formal diarrhea

General Use diarrhea, loose bowels

Slang the runs, the trots, the quickstep, Montezuma's revenge, turistas

Vulgar Hershey squirts, the shits

• • •

Formal constipation, be constipated

General Use constipation, be irregular

Euphemism irregularity, be irregular, unable to go

Children's Words can't poop, can't ka ka

Slang stuck, blocked up

Vulgar shitting a brick

• • •

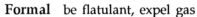

Formal be flatulant, expel gas

General Use expel gas, pass gas

Euphemism pass wind, break wind

Children's Words make poops, go oops, poop

Slang back talk, beep, blow the horn, buck snort, let one out, let out a stinker, let out a whiffer, winder, toot

Vulgar blow a fart, blow one, cut a fart, cut one, let out an S. B. D. (silent but deadly), rip one

• • •

Formal urinate, empty one's bladder, void

General Use urinate

Euphemism relieve oneself, pass water, make water, go to the bathroom

Children's Words do, go, or make: number one, pee pee, wee wee; go potty, make a river, pish, go pishie, tinkle

Slang check the plumbing, drain a vein, water the lilies

Vulgar leak, pee, piss, take a leak, take a piss, take a leak, take a piss, shake hands with a friend, water one's pony

• • •

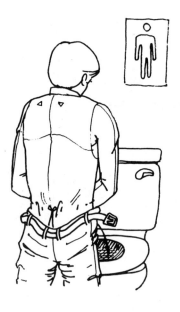

Formal   menstruate (women only)

General Use   have one's period

Euphemism   be unwell (old fashioned)

Slang   have a visit from Aunt Minnie, Fall off the roof, have one's friend, have the curse

Vulgar   have the rag on, ride the cotton pony

E.   In the Bedroom

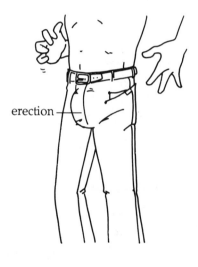

erection

Formal   (male) have an erection, be erect

General Use   be aroused, be excited

Euphemism   be in the mood, be interested, be ready

Slang   be hot, be hot to trot, have the hots, be turned on

Vulgar   be horny, have a hard-on, be hard, be stiff, have a boner

•   •   •

Formal   (female) be lubricating

General Use   be aroused, be excited

Euphemism   be in the mood, be interested, be ready

Slang   be juicy, be wet, be hot to trot, be turned on

Vulgar   be horny

•   •   •

Formal copulate (with), have coitus, have (sexual) intercourse, engage in sexual intercourse

General Use have (sexual) relations, have sex, make love, mate (with)

Euphemism go to bed with, sleep with, have contact with, go all the way, have carnal knowledge of, know, be intimate with, couple, enjoy each other, possess

Slang diddle, do it, get a little, get some nookie, get some action, get it on, have some, make (a person), make it with, mess around, play hide the sausage

Vulgar ball, bang, frig, fuck, get into her pants, get laid, get one's end wet, get a piece of ass, get some ass, get some nookie, get some poon tang, hump, lay, schtup, screw, shaft, tear off a piece

• • •

Formal achieve orgasm, reach a sexual climax, ejaculate (male)

General Use have a climax, have an orgasm

Euphemism be satisfied, finish, "the earth moved"

Vulgar come, cream, drop one's load, get one's nuts off, get one's rocks off, give a shot, shoot off, shoot one's wad

• • •

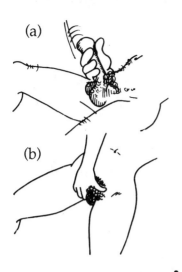

(a)

(b)

Formal masturbate (male or female)

General Use masturbate

Euphemism satisfy oneself, abuse oneself

Slang diddle, play with oneself, see Madam Hand and her five daughters

Vulgar (male uses) beat the meat, beat off, choke the chicken, flog one's dong, fuck one's fist, jack off, jerk off, whack off, yank off

• • •

Formal oral-genital sex (both sexes), fellatio (mouth to male genitals), cunnilingus (mouth to female genitals

General Use oral sex

Euphemism go down on

Slang sixty-nine, soixante-neuf

Vulgar blow, eat, give a blow job, give head, go muff diving, have hair pie, suck, suck cock

• • •

Formal anal sex, sodomy

General Use anal sex

Euphemism the Greek way

Slang use the back door, go up the old dirt road

Vulgar ass-fuck, bugger, use the shit chute

• • •

Formal impregnate

General Use make pregnant

Euphemism get with child, get a girl in trouble

Slang plant a watermelon seed in her belly

Vulgar knock up

• • •

Formal   pregnant, gestating

General Use   pregnant

Euphemism   great with child, in a family way, expecting a child

Slang   preggers, swallowed a watermelon seed, have one in the oven, cooking one in the pot

Vulgar   knocked up

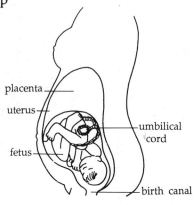

• • •

Formal   (use) contraception, contraceptive devices

General Use   (use) birth control

Euphemism   be safe, be careful, (take) preventive measures, (take) precautions

Slang   make the playground safe for play

• • •

condom

Formal   condom, prophylactic

General Use   condom

Euphemism   safety, pro

Slang   baggie, diving suit, envelope, French letter, glove, helmet, overcoat, raincoat, rubber

Vulgar   scum bag

• • •

D. On the Street

Formal heterosexual

Slang straight

• • •

Formal prostitute

General Use prostitute, street walker, call girl

Euphemism lady of the night, lady of easy virtue

Slang flesh peddler, harlot, hooker, hustler, tart, paid lady, princess of the pavement, working girl

Vulgar whore, ass peddler, cunt-for-sale, slut

• • •

Formal male prostitute

General Use gigolo

Euphemism escort service

• • •

Formal house of prostitution

General Use house of prostitution, brothel

Euphemism bordello, disorderly house, house of ill-repute, house of pleasure, joy house, massage parlor, red-light district

Slang bawdy house, cat house, flesh market, meat house, nunnery, sporting house

Vulgar fuckery, fuck house, whorehouse

• • •

Formal   homosexual (either sex), lesbian (female)

General Use   gay (either sex), homosexual (male), lesbian (female)

Euphemism   the third sex

Slang   (derogatory) homo, neuter gender, person of indeterminate gender; (derogatory, male) queer, queen, fairy, fruit, pansy; (derogatory, female) butch, dyke, bulldyke, lezzie

Vulgar   cocksucker, buggerer (male), dick smoker, fudge packer, pickle chuggler, salami smuggler (all derogatory)

• • •

Formal   male prostitute (homosexual)

Slang   chicken

Dangerous People: Perverts and Perversions

sadist
dominatrix

exhibitionist
(flasher)

A *perversion* is a sexual act that is not "normal." There are religious rules against "non-normal" sex practices. There are laws, too, in some states. A *pervert* is a person who engages in "non-normal" sex acts.

But the law does not reach in to people's bedrooms. In today's society in America, *consenting adults* may engage in any sex practice they choose in the *privacy* of their bedrooms. (Consenting = giving permission freely, not forced; adults = persons over 18 years of age; in privacy = alone, not in public.)

The following terms for various sexual deviations will be found defined in the Definitions section.

bestiality		
exhibitionism	exhibitionist	flasher
fetishism	fetishist	
molestation	molester	child molester
masochism	masochist	
necrophilia	necrophiliac	
pederasty	pederast	
pedophilia	pedophiliac	
rape	rapist	
sadism	sadist	sadomasochism
sodomy	sodomist	buggerer
transvestism	transvestite	
voyeurism	voyeur	peeping Tom

Dangers in the Doctor's Office

The pages that follow are written by an English teacher, not a doctor. It is language information, not medical advice.

A. Females

Women's bodies contain complex "plumbing." When a woman has *"female complaints,"* the doctor she goes to see is a *gynecologist*.

Obstetrics is the specialty of doctors who care for women during pregnancy, and assist at the baby's delivery. Most *gynecologists* are also *obstetricians*. Some women prefer to have a baby born at home. A *midwife* helps with home deliveries.

A girl normally enters *puberty* between the ages of ten and fifteen. She begins to *menstruate* and develop *secondary sex characteristics:* breasts, hair in the *pubic* and underarm regions, and wider hips. The female *hormones* — *estrogen* and *progesterone* — cause body changes.

Each month, an *ovum* (egg) leaves the *ovary*. It passes through the *fallopian tubes* to the *uterus*, and out of the *vagina*. The thick lining of the *uterus* is let go, and *menstruation* occurs. The woman says she is *having her period*.

Problems that some women have are *heavy flow, menstrual cramps*, and an *irregular cycle*. Some women experience *PMS* (Pre-Menstrual Syndrome) for a few days before their *period*.

A woman will use a *sanitary napkin* to catch the *flow* or insert a *tampon* into the vagina. *Toxic shock syndrome* is a rare, but very dangerous condition. It can be caused by bacteria that build in the vagina or uterus during menstruation when the woman uses tampons.

Before her first sexual experience, a girl is a *virgin*. A virgin has a *hymen* or membrane that partly covers the opening to the *vagina*. This will stretch or break during her first sexual *intercourse*. Sometimes it will break before this when she is playing a fast game of tennis or some other activity.

A *gynecological* examination will include a breast examination and a *pelvic* examination. The doctor may also do a *Pap smear*, take a *specimen* for *urinalysis*, and check for *venereal disease*. If there is a *vaginal itch*, *vaginal discharge*, or other signs of *vaginitis*, the doctor may check for *VD* (venereal disease), *trichomoniasis* ("trich"), *monilia*, or other *yeast-type infections*. He may recommend medication, a change in diet, or a *douche*. The doctor should teach the woman how to do a *breast self-examination* to feel for *lumps* that might be *cancer*.

When a girl or woman becomes *sexually active*, she will want to ask the gynecologist about *birth control*, or *contraception*. The doctor may recommend *"the pill,"* a *diaphragm*, *spermicidal foam*, or an *intrauterine device*. He will explain that *douching* is not effective, nor is *coitus interruptus* ("withdrawal"). If she is Catholic, the doctor will explain the *rhythm method* of birth control.

So far, the only 100% effective methods of birth control are *abstinence* and *sterilization*. If a woman has already had several children, she may think about "having her tubes tied." This is called a *tubal ligation*, in which the *fallopian tubes* are cut or sealed closed, so the egg cannot reach the uterus.

If she has *painful intercourse*, the doctor may advise a *lubricant* such as *K-Y Jelly*.

If the ovum is *fertilized* by a man's *sperm*, it begins to grow and attaches itself to the lining of the uterus. The woman *misses her period*, which is the first sign that she is *pregnant*. Another early sign may be *"morning sickness."* The *fetus*, or unborn child, will *gestate* for nine months. One in six pregnancies ends in *miscarriage* (spontaneous abortion).

The law presently allows a woman to end her pregnancy with a *medical abortion* during the early months. There is a lot of disagreement about this. The laws may have been changed when you read this book.

Labor contractions begin when the baby is ready to be born. Just before birth, the doctor may cut the woman's *perineum*, which is the area between the vagina and the anus. This cut is called an *episiotomy*. After the birth, the *episiotomy* is sewn, and the *stitches* will be removed or absorbed in a few days. If the birth is very difficult, the doctor may decide to do a *caesarian section.*

After the baby is born, the mother may *breast-feed* it or bottle-feed it. She may do *Kegel exercises* to strengthen the muscles in her vagina.

A married couple who are unable to *conceive* may go to an *infertility* clinic. The doctor's there may recommend *hormone therapy, artificial insemination,* or the use of a *sperm donor.*

Some other concerns of women are intermittent *bleeding, staining, and painful ovulation.* Women also may have *endometriosis,* burning during urination, and *hormonal imbalances. Fibrocystic* breast conditions are normal in many mature women, but can be painful, or confused with cancer. A *mammograph* is a test for breast cancer. If cancer exists, a woman may need a *mastectomy* (removal of the breast) or a *lumpectomy.* (Removal of the lump or tumor.)

When the childbearing years are over, a woman's ovaries stop producing *estrogen,* and she undergoes *menopause,* or the *"change of life."* Her periods become *irregular,* and then stop. She may have *hot flashes.* Some doctors recommend *estrogen replacement therapy,* or *hormone treatments* for difficulties that may come with menopause.

Post-menopausal bleeding can be serious. Sometimes all that is needed is a *"D and C."* (Dilation and curettage, in which the gynecologist cleans the lining of the uterus.) There may be a need for a *hysterectomy,* or removal of the uterus by surgery. Women are advised to always get a *second opinion.* (Consult a second or even a third doctor.)

B. Males

A family doctor can examine and treat many male medical conditions. For special cases a man might go to a *urologist.*

Today, many boy babies are *circumcised,* which means that part of the *foreskin* of the penis is cut. This makes it easier to clean the *smegma* around the head of the penis.

A boy undergoes *puberty* between the ages of eleven and sixteen. His *testes* produce *testosterone,* a male *hormone.* This causes muscle growth, a deep voice, a beard, and hair in the *pubic area* and armpits. He may begin to have *nocturnal emissions* at this age.

Problems that can bring a boy or man to a doctor are *undescended testicles,* "jock itch," difficulty when *urinating,* blood in the urine, or a swollen *scrotum.* *Kidney stones* cause pain when they are passed from the kidneys to the *bladder,* or from the bladder through the *urethra.*

A man can get a *hernia,* or *rupture,* when he lifts or pushes a very heavy weight. A part of the intestine protrudes into the testicle. This may need surgery to repair.

Sexual difficulties may be *impotence, painful erection, performance anxiety, premature ejaculation,* or *sterility.*

A *catheter* may be needed when there is difficulty *urinating.* This goes through the *urethra* to the bladder. A *cystoscope* allows a doctor to look into the bladder.

Prostatitis is an inflammation of the prostate. The doctor may do a rectal examination to check the *prostate gland.* He may *palpate* or massage the prostate, which will cause *ejaculation.*

C. Males and Females

The doctor who treats problems of the lower digestive tract is a *proctologist.*

After digestion, the waste material passes from the *colon* and is stored in the *rectum.* When the rectum is full, contractions push the *fecal matter* out through the *anus.*

Common conditions and complaints of the colon, rectum, and anus are: *hemorrhoids, constipation, cramps, diarrhea,* and *colitis.* A patient may have *diverticulosis,* which can turn into *diverticulitis.*

To diagnose the condition, the doctor may do a *sigmoidoscopy.* This means putting a long, flexible instrument into the rectum in order to look inside the colon. He may take X-rays after the patient has had a *barium enema.*

Other problems may be *rectal fissures, fistula, rectocele,* and *rectal prolapse.*

D. Sexually Transmitted Diseases (STD's)

There are many forms of *venereal disease*, or VD. Some can be cured. Some can be treated, but not cured. The worst is *AIDS* (acquired immunodeficiency syndrome).

Gonorrhea, syphilis, and *chlamydia* are gotten through sexual contact. *Genital herpes* may be gotten through sexual contact, or through toilet seats, using the same wash cloth or towel, or bed linens. AIDS is gotten through intercourse, (particularly *anal* intercourse) from sharing intravenous needles, or blood transfusions.

Genital warts can be transmitted to a partner and should be treated.

Some *yeast infections* are transmitted sexually.

Pubic lice, or *crabs,* can be spread by sexual contact. But you can also get them from a toilet seat, from using the same towels, or sharing the same bed.

Religious Taboos

One of the laws in Jewish/Christian religion is that "You may not take the name of God in vain." That is, you may say the words "God" and "Jesus" when praying, or speaking about them, but you may not say these words for nonreligious reasons.

Very religious people consider that it is a sin to use the following expressions to express anger or other strong emotions. *Blasphemy* is the sin of using the name of God in a dishonorable way.

Christ!	God!
For Christ's sake!	God damn it!
Christ Almighty!	Hell!
Jesus!	Go to Hell!
Jesus Christ!	

Religious people carefully avoid saying these words. However, the words are heard continuously in all-male groups and on work teams, and are very common among many others groups, including informal mixed groups.

In mixed company, some people soften the words. They say other words that begin with the same sounds.

Cripes!	Gosh!
Christmas!	Cheese and crackers!
For crying out loud!	Goldarnit!
Gee Whiz!	Heck!
Golly!	Go to Heck!

Correct Your Dangerous Pronunciation

A foreign accent can often cause problems in understanding. Occasionally, your accent can cause major embarrassment if your mispronunciation results in a dangerous word.

If you are from Europe or Latin America, you may have difficulty with American vowel sounds. It is especially difficult to distinguish the "long ē" (as in hē) from "short ĭ" (as in hĭm). This means that words like shĭp  and shēep, may be pronounced to sound almost the same.

Sentences such as, "I went to Bermuda by (shēp)," or "We saw a (shĭp) near the cow," may cause slight smiles among the Americans who are listening.

However...

It can be *very* embarrassing if you confuse the sound of *shēet* (a cloth covering for a bed) and *shĭt* (feces).

"I put some clean shits on the bed."

Difficulty in pronouncing other English vowels may be responsible for embarrassment if you are not careful:

Acceptable word that *you want to say*	Sexual or bathroom-related word that may result from *mispronouncing it*
beach (bēch)	bitch (bĭch)
piece (pēs)	piss (pĭs)
shirt (shurt)	shit (shĭt)
six (sĭks)	sex (sĕks)
fog (fŏg)	fuck (fŭk)
fork (fork)	fuck (fŭk)
folks (fōks)	fucks (fŭks)

"Do you mind if I take a pis?"

The /th/ sound is difficult for almost all foreign-born people. This is because the sound does not exist in most other languages.

To correctly pronounce /th/, slightly stick out your tongue between the upper and lower front teeth. Gently force the air out between the tongue and the upper teeth.

Acceptable Pronunciation	Embarrassing Mispronunciation
third (thurd)	turd (turd)
farther (far´ <u>th</u>ur)	farter (far´ tur)
theses (thē ´ sēs)	feces (fē´ sēs)

Some Oriental languages, including Japanese and Chinese, do not have the distinction between the sounds /l/ and /r/. This makes it very hard for those speakers to make an English /l/ or /r/ that sounds right to Americans.

Acceptable	Embarrassing
ray	lay
rust	lust
rude	lewd
clap	crap
election	erection

"The audience crapped for a long time after the concert."

The difficulty that Japanese speakers have in pronouncing the English /l/ is so well known that there is a common joke about it.

If a man is a candidate for some public office or is hoping to win some position or honor, a friend may say to him, "Lots of luck on your coming election." But he will say it with his hands folded in front of him and bow as though he were Japanese, and imitate a Japanese accent. Then he will sound like this: "Rots of ruck on your coming erection."

"Rots of ruck on your coming erection."

Koreans and some Japanese have difficulty with the simple /s/ sound before a short /i/ sound. Watch out!

Acceptable	Embarrassing
New York City	New York shitty
Please sit down	Please shit down
University	Univershitty

If you have any of these pronunciation problems, we hope that you will now see how important it can be to correct them!

Safe and Dangerous Words for Races, Religions, or Nationalities

People of many different races and national backgrounds live in the United States. Marriages, friendships, and business partnerships between people from different national backgrounds or religions are very common. Many Americans are "mixtures" of two, four, or eight different ethnic groups, and are proud of it.

Our national ideals tell us to judge others as individuals, not as members of a race or group. National laws prohibit discrimination based on race or national group.

The "real" has not yet equalled the "ideal." One sign of this is the slang terms that people use to talk about other groups. While some of the slang terms are intended to be humorous, most of them are derogatory. Many terms are extremely offensive. Someone hearing these terms about his race or group may become angry enough to fight.

The visitor or foreign student in the United States should learn the correct and acceptable terms for the various national and racial groups. If you use the slang terms you may be marked as a bigot (an ignorant or intolerant person).

A member of a group may humorously use a slang term for his *own* group, but will find it offensive for someone else to use the word.

Many minority groups are adopting new terms to label themselves. Older terms are now becoming offensive to some. By the time you read this book, some of these terms may change. Hopefully someday people will say, "There is only one race, and that's the human race; we are all citizens of one planet."

Warning: In the slang terms in this list, you will find some of the most dangerous and offensive English words of all.

1. **American** (acceptable) People in the United States call themselves *Americans.* However, Central and South Americans are also Americans, and refer to people from the United States as *North Americans.* But the term North American includes Canadians and Mexicans. There is no other single word that means a person who is a citizen of the United States.

   U.S. Citizen (acceptable)

   Yankee (slang, not offensive to Americans, although it may be said in a derogatory way by people in other countries, i.e.,"Yankee go home.") Americans use it to refer to themselves with some pride. "New York Yankees," "Yankee pot roast," "Yankee know-how." A second meaning of *Yankee* is "Northerner," and in this sense, it may be derogatory when spoken by a person from the South.

   Gringo (mildly derogatory. Mexican and Southwestern use) Any non-Mexican, non-Spanish speaker, but especially American. Usually accepted with good humor by Americans who are labeled "Gringo."

   Anglo (acceptable) Used by governments and educators to refer to English-Speaking Americans. It contrasts with L.E.P. or Limited English Proficient speakers.

2. **Arab** (ă´ rĭb) (acceptable) A person from any Arabic speaking country.

   Ayrab (ā´ răb´) (derogatory)

3. **Asian** (ā´ zhĕn) (acceptable) This term correctly refers to all people of the continent of Asia. It is sometimes used to refer only to those of the Mongolian race, such as Chinese, Korean, Japanese, Vietnamese, etc.

   The term *Oriental* was formerly correct, but is going out of fashion.

   Gook (extremely offensive)

   Slant (extremely offensive)

4. **African-American** (acceptable) This term refers to people whose ancestors came from Africa. It is replacing the term Black. About 12 percent of Americans are African-Americans. Also, *Afro-Americans*.

Black (acceptable) This was the preferred term from the 1960's to the time of this revision. It is being replaced by *African-Americans*.

Blood (slang) Used by African-Americans to refer to other African-Americans. Short for *Blood Brother*.

Boy (derogatory) Extremely offensive when used by a white person speaking to an adult African-American.

Brother (slang) Short for *Blood Brother, Soul Brother*. Used by African-Americans for each other.

Sister (slang) Short for *Soul Sister*. See above.

Negro (acceptable, but not preferred) Widely used by older people.

Colored (considered by some to be derogatory) Out of fashion. Still in use by older people.

Coon (slang. extremely offensive)

Nigger (extremely offensive) The use of this term by a member of another race has caused violence.

Spade (slang. offensive)

Spook (slang. offensive)

5. **British** (acceptable) Person from Great Britain

English (acceptable)

Limey (lī´ mē) (humorous)

WASP (*W*hite *A*nglo-*S*axon *P*rotestant; acceptable or derogatory, depending on the context and who is speaking)

Anglo-Saxon Of English or German origin

---

6. **Chicano** (chĭ ka´ nō) (acceptable) Americans of Mexican background, particularly in Texas, California, New Mexico, and Arizona.

   Mex (slang. derogatory)

   Mexican-American (acceptable) Refers to people who have come to the U.S. from Mexico.

   Spic (derogatory) Spanish-speakers, especially in the North East.

   Hispanic (hĭs păn´ ĭk) (acceptable) Any person who speaks Spanish, or identifies with Central and South Americans or Spanish from Spain.

   Latin (acceptable) A person from Latin American background. This may include Portuguese speakers from Brazil.

   Puerto Rican (acceptable) Puerto Ricans are American citizens.

   P.R. (slang. less acceptable)

   Spanish (acceptable) A person from Spain. Less correct: A person who speaks Spanish, no matter where he or she is from. It is better to refer to the exact nationality, or use the term *Hispanic*.

7. **Chinese** (acceptable) Refers to people of Chinese background and recent immigrants from mainland China.

   Taiwanese (acceptable) Chinese from Taiwan use this to distinguish themselves from persons from Communist mainland China.

   Chinaman (slang. mildly derogatory)

   Chink (slang. derogatory)

8. **French** (acceptable)

   Frog (humorous or mildly derogatory)

9. **Canadian** (acceptable)

   French-Canadian (acceptable)

   Canuck (kŭ nŭk´) (slang. sometimes derogatory)

10. **German-American** (acceptable)

    Kraut (humorous, sometimes derogatory)

    Heinie (hī´ nē) (derogatory)

11. **Hungarian** (acceptable)

    Hunkie (slang. derogatory)

12. **Indo-Chinese** (acceptable) Includes people from Vietnam, Laos, Cambodia, Thailand, Burma.

    Slant (extremely offensive)

    Gook (extremely offensive)

14. **Irish-American** (acceptable)

    Irisher (slang. derogatory)

    Mick (slang. derogatory)

    Paddy (slang. derogatory)

15. **Italian-American** (acceptable)

    Dago (dā´ gō) (derogatory)

    Wop (derogatory)

    Guinea, Guinny, Ginnie (gĭ´ nē) (derogatory)

---

16. **Japanese** (acceptable)

   Jap (derogatory)

   Nip (derogatory)

17. **Jew, Jewish** (acceptable)

   Kike (kīk) (derogatory)

   Jewboy (derogatory)

   Hebe (hēb) (derogatory)

   Ikey (ī´ kē) (derogatory)

   Sheeny (derogatory)

   Yid (derogatory)

18. **Gentile** (acceptable) A term used by Jews for non-Jews.

   Goy, (plural - goyim) (derogatory) Non-Jews

   Shagits A non-Jewish man (derogatory)

   Schikse A non-Jewish woman (derogatory)

19. **Native American** (acceptable) A person descended from any of the native tribes in America before Europeans arrived.

   Indian (less acceptable) Since Columbus though he was in India, he wrongly named the Native Americans "Indians." They have renamed themselves Native Americans. However, the word *Indian* is difficult to erase from the language and literature after such a long history.

   Injin (slang. less acceptable)

   Redskin (derogatory)

20. **Polish-American** (acceptable)

Polack (pō´ lŏk) (derogatory)

21. **White** (acceptable)

Caucasian (kaw kā´ zhŭn) (acceptable, formal) A member of the "White" race.

Honkie (derogatory) Used by African-Americans.

Whitie (derogatory)

Fay (derogatory)

The Man (derogatory)

White Trash (derogatory)

Cracker (derogatory) White Southerner.

Vanilla (humorous) Used by African-Americans.

22. **Person of mixed parentage** (acceptable) Refers to a person whose parents were of different races: Black/White; Black/Asian; Black/Native American; White/Asian; White/Native American.

Half-breed (derogatory) Refers to any of the above combinations.

Zebra (derogatory) Having one Black and one White parent.

Mulatto (mŭ lŏt´ ō) (less acceptable) Having Black and White Blood.

High Yaller (yellow) (slang. derogatory) A light-skinned African-American.

Dangerous Body Language

A. Personal Space

There are many differences in nonverbal communication as well as in speech in a new language.

We don't often think about it, but we all have a certain feeling about the space surrounding our bodies. We try to keep a certain distance from people when we are talking to them. We don't like people to come closer than this, or to be father away. This personal distance is different in different places in the world.

An American stands about twenty-four inches (arm's length) from the person he or she is talking to. This is the "comfort zone" for conversation. If you come closer, the American may step backward in order to keep this comfortable distance between you. The need for this personal space is part of our culture, but it is not part of our conscious thinking.

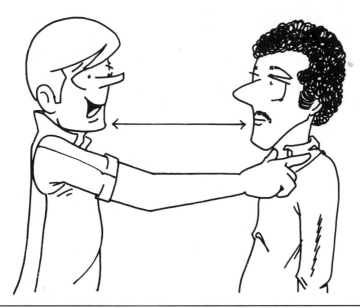

If you are from a culture where people stand closer together when they are speaking, you may feel that the American is rude for moving away. The American may feel that you are getting "too personal and intimate" if you move closer.

A man may move closer than arm's length to a woman when he is sexually interested in her. If she is interested, she does not step back. If she is not interested, she steps back. Try to stand at the "correct" distance so the person you are talking to does not get the wrong idea about your intentions.

On the other hand, if you are from a culture where people have a wider "personal space," you may prefer to talk to people at a distance of thirty inches. An American will step closer to you to stay at *his* or *her* most comfortable distance. You may automatically step backward and the American may think you are "cold, distant, or unfriendly." If the American steps toward you again, you may think he or she is too aggressive, or perhaps making a sexual advance. Both of you will be mistaken.

B. Touching

Touching also has different meanings in different cultures. Even Americans misinterpret each other, because there is a great variety of regional, ethnic, and personal behavior. It is impossible to make statements that will be true in every case. You should observe the touching behavior that goes on around you before you "speak" this nonverbal language.

Compared to Asians and some Northern Europeans, Americans are more likely to touch each other and show affection in public. Compared to Southern Europeans and South Americans, they are "cooler," and seem to keep at a distance. So your impression will be based on the culture that you come from.

Many women generally hug close friends when greeting them if it has been a long time since they last saw them. A woman may hug a friend (male or female) to congratulate him or her on a birthday, graduation, or good news. Friends may hug to give or receive thanks for a gift or a favor. The hugs between women and women or between women and men may be accompanied by a light kiss on the cheek or a brief "smack" (kiss) on the lips (or in the air between the two pairs of lips!). Usually, nothing sexual is intended in these hugs, and a quick kiss of this sort should not be interpreted as a sexual act or invitation.

Other American women do not hug or kiss or wish to be embraced or kissed on such occasions.

Men generally shake hands with male friends to say hello when they have not seen them for a long time. They may also give a firm pat on the shoulder or slap on the upper back. Men shake hands when they are introduced to other men. A firm handshake is considered a sign of good character. A weak handshake is considered unmasculine.

In business, women offer to shake hands when they are introduced to others. In social situations, it is not necessary for women to shake hands. Women, too, should have a firm handshake. *Avoid shaking hands like a "dead fish."* Ask Americans to show you the proper handshake grip, if you are in doubt.

Men embrace female friends whom they haven't seen for a long time, and they may embrace them to offer congratulations or thanks for a gift.

Men do not usually hug other men, except family members, although they may clasp shoulders to show friendship or sympathy. There are great ethnic and personal variations in hugging. There are many exceptions to any rules that might be given. Observe the behavior of men and women around you.

Here are some generalizations, with many exceptions:

People from Mediterranean origins (Italian, French, Greek, Spanish, and Latin Americans) generally touch more in public, and show more affection in public. They use their hands a lot when they speak. They are likely to touch you while talking to you.

If you are in California, you can expect to see more people hugging each other than you would on the East Coast. They may hug each other hello and goodbye, even on a first meeting.

Teachers in elementary school frequently hug the younger students.

People of Asian backgrounds or Northern European backgrounds (German, English, Norwegian, Swedish, etc.) are more "reserved." They show less affection in public.

Magazine articles are frequently written about the benefits of hugging to encourage people to hug their friends and family members. One article said, "Four hugs a day is the minimum daily requirement, eight is better, and twelve hugs will make sure we stay in the best of health.

Public kissing by two people who are "in love" or are attracted to each other is quite common. A couple may walk down the street holding hands or have their arms around each other. In certain areas of large cities, or in certain bars or clubs, homosexual couples may also hold hands, hug, and kiss. This is unusual in most other areas. Passionate kissing in public is offensive to some people.

A woman may hold hands or walk with an arm around another woman if she is a sister or a very close friend. In America, if men hold hands or kiss, people may assume that they have a homosexual relationship.

C. Gestures

There are many nonverbal gestures used by Americans. Some of these are vulgar, and are translated into vulgar language.

A strong insult is given by children and others with the "nose salute." Sometimes this is accompanied by sticking out the tongue, and wiggling the four fingers. Translation: Anger, hatred, lack of respect. An adult equivalent might be "Kiss my ass."

The most common vulgar gesture is "giving the finger." The translation of this is "up your ass," "up yours" or "sit on this." It is used to show contempt, anger, or hatred. The middle finger is extended, and the other fingers are folded. The hand is waved upward at the other person, with the back of the hand facing the observer.

The middle finger should not be used to point with, or to count "one" with. It will look as though you are "giving someone the finger."

A gesture that came into English usage through Italian body language is the "arm-crack." This is done by placing the left wrist inside the bent forearm of the right arm. The right arm is brought quickly backwards, folding over the left. The translation is "Fuck you."

Dangerous Definitions and Sample Sentences

This section will be easier to use if you first learn the *formal* words that are illustrated in the *synonyms* section. Many definitions will refer to these correct terms.

In a book of this size, we cannot include *every single* medical, slang, or vulgar word for sexual or toilet activities. (One researcher found over 1,200 words for sexual intercourse alone!) We have chosen over 700 of the words and expressions you are most likely to hear, or need to use. These are words that are commonly known by many Americans.

To save space, we do not give every possible meaning for each word. We include *only* the meanings that are related to sex and toilet acts and functions, expressions that include these words, and some expressions forbidden by church teachings.

For example, a standard dictionary gives 28 meanings for the word *head*, many of which you already know. In this book, we explain only the sex-related slang and vulgar meanings.

If a word has other, nonsexual, non-toilet meanings, we have marked the word with a star (*). If you don't already know the common meaning of the word, you may look it up in a standard dictionary or your bilingual dictionary.

The meaning of many slang and vulgar expressions depends on the context. Some words spoken with affection or humor can mean something very different from the same words spoken in anger. A lot depends on who is speaking, to whom the words are spoken, and how they are spoken.

a

* **abstinence** (ăb´ stĭ nĕns)   noun, from the verb *abstain*.
formal, general use.   Not having sexual relations. It is a
personal choice. "*Abstinence* is becoming more popular with
single people today because of the fear of AIDS."

* **accident** (ăk´ sĭ dĕnt)   noun.   1. slang euphemism. An
unplanned baby. A failure of birth control. "Our first child
was planned, but the other two were *accidents*." 2. euphemism.
A bowel movement or urinating in one's pants. "Our three-
year-old daughter has been out of diapers for six months, but
she has an *accident* now and then."

* **a.c./d.c.** (ā´ sē dē´ sē)   adjective. slang.   Bisexual. Said of
a person who has sexual relations with both men *and* women.
(The reference is to two different kinds of electrical current:
alternating current and direct current.)

* **adult** (ŭ dŭlt´)   adjective. euphemism.   When the word
adult is used in such expressions as *adult book store, adult movies,*
and *adult entertainment*, it has the meaning: for adults only,
because they contain pornographic material. (The subject of the
book, movies or show is sexual activities. The purpose is to
create sexual excitement in the reader or audience. Or they
may contain words that are vulgar) (*Adult education* does not
have this meaning!)

adultery (ŭ dŭl´ tur ē)   noun. formal, legal, general use.
The act of sexual intercourse between a man and a woman who
are not married to each other. One or both partners is married
to someone else. The word implies the judgement that the act
is wrong, or criminal. "*Adultery* is a sin, according to Christian
teachings." "Mrs. C. wanted a divorce because her husband had
committed adultery."

adulterer (ŭ dŭl´ tur ur)   noun. formal.   A person who
commits adultery.

adulteress (ŭ dŭl´ trĭs)   noun. formal.   A woman who
commits adultery.

adulterous (ŭ dŭl´ tur ŭs)   adjective. formal.   "Mr. A.
was guilty of *adulterous* behavior." The words *adultery, adulterer,
adulteress,* and *adulterous* have no connection in meaning with
the word *adult.*

---

* **affair** (ŭ fār´) noun. general use. A relationship between a man and a woman who are not married to each other. The relationship includes sex, and may continue for a period of weeks, months, or years. Either partner may be married to someone else. The word does not imply judgement of evil or wrong-doing. "A. had many *affairs* before she got married." "Harry was having an *affair* with his secretary, but his wife didn't know about it."

AIDS (ādz) noun. formal, general use. A very serious disease, *A*cquired *I*mmune *D*eficiency *S*yndrome. Many victims are male homosexuals, but other men and women can get AIDS. It can be spread through contact with the blood of someone with AIDS. People can be infected with the AIDS virus and not know it for years. Drug addicts who share needles with AIDS infected carriers and people who receive blood transfusions from AIDS carriers will get the AIDS virus. Babies born to mothers with AIDS also have AIDS.

A.K. noun. 1. euphemism for the vulgar Ass-Kisser (below). 2. Alte Koche. vulgar. Yiddish expression. Old shitter. A "dirty old man" who likes to romance pretty young women.

* **alley cat** noun. slang. A man or woman who has casual sexual relations with many people. "N. was a real *alley cat* before he got married, but he's been faithful to his wife."

* **all the way** adverbial phrase. Euphemism commonly used by teenagers. To go "all the way" means to have complete sexual intercourse. *Half-way* may mean kissing, necking, and petting (touching the genitals). "C. was afraid of getting pregnant so she never went *all the way* with a boy."

* **altar** (awl´ tur) noun. slang. The toilet.

* **alter** (awl´ tur) adverbial phrase. euphemism. To castrate a male animal or spay a female animal. To remove the sex glands of a cat or dog so it cannot reproduce. "We had our cat *altered*."

* **altogether, in the** phrase. slang euphemism. Naked; with no clothes on. "She took off her wet clothes and stood by the fire *in the altogether*."

anus (ā´ nŭs) noun. formal, medical use. The exit hole of the rectum. "The feces (digestive waste material) are pushed out of the body through the *anus*."

anal sex (ā´ nŭl sĕks) noun. formal. Sexual intercourse through the anus or rectal opening.

A.R.C. AIDS-Related Complex.

* **arouse** (ŭ rou´z) verb. general use. Cause someone to become sexually excited. "R.'s gentle kisses *aroused* M." "Some men get *aroused* when they see bare breasts."

arse (ars) noun. vulgar. A variant form of *ass*. The buttocks.

ass (ăs) noun. general use. A foolish person. This is from the word jackass, a male donkey. *This* use of the word is not considered vulgar.

ass noun. vulgar. 1. The buttocks. 2. The rectum. 3. The anus. 4. The vagina.

ass-backwards (ăs´ băk´ wurdz) adjective, adverb. vulgar. Backwards, all mixed up. Done in a confused way. Also *Back-assward*. "These directions are all *ass-backwards*; I can't understand what to do."

ass hole (ăs´ hōl´) noun. vulgar. 1. The anus. 2. A stupid and incompetent person.

ass-hole buddy (ăs´ hōl´ bŭd´ ē) noun. vulgar. A very close friend. (not homosexual, as the term might make you think.) "Roger, George, Sam, and I were *ass-hole buddies* all through college."

ass, to haul (hawl´ ăs´) verb phrase. vulgar. To hurry.

ass, to kick verb phrase. vulgar. To get tough; threaten people, demanding change in behavior or rapid work. "To be a sergeant in the army, you have to be good at *kicking ass*."

ass-kisser noun. vulgar. A person who is overly nice to his boss, teachers, or superiors in order to get special privileges, good marks, or favors. "R. is the biggest *ass-kisser* I know. He's always asking if there is any more work he can do, and telling the boss what a great boss he is."

ass, to kiss verb. vulgar. To continually compliment and do favors for a superior, hoping for a promotion, good marks in class, or special favors. "You don't have to know anything in Professor T.'s class. All you have to do is *kiss ass*: tell him how much you love his teaching style, and how interesting his course is."

ass! , kiss my vulgar. No, I certainly won't do what you asked. "H. asked me to lend him money again, and I told him to *kiss my ass*."

ass man   noun. vulgar.   A man who is attracted to women with large firm buttocks. He finds the buttocks to be the most sexually attractive part of a woman. 2. A man who is constantly interested in sex, in finding new sex partners, and in talking about his sexual adventures.

ass peddler   noun. vulgar.   A prostitute (male or female). To *peddle one's ass* is to sell sexual services. "D. came to the big city to become an actress, but she wound up *peddling her ass.*"

ass-wipe   (ăs´ wīp´)   noun. vulgar.   1. Toilet paper. 2. A very stupid person.

*There are many other expressions that include the word **ass**.*

bare-ass, bare-assed   (băr ăs, băr ăst)   adjective. vulgar. Completely naked. With no clothes on.   "The boys went swimming *bare-ass.*" "He opened the dressing-room door and caught her *bare-assed.*"

bust one's ass   verb phrase. vulgar.   1. To work very hard to accomplish a goal. "L. *busted his ass* to finish the job before Friday." 2. Punish by forcefully spanking the buttocks. "If you do that again, I'll '*bust your ass!*' shouted the angry mother to the child."

dumb ass   (dŭm´ ăs´)   noun phrase. vulgar.   A stupid person.

get one's ass in gear   verb phrase. vulgar.   To get organized. "We made a lot of mistakes at first, but as soon as we *got our ass in gear*, we got results."

half-assed   adjective. vulgar.   1. Done in a sloppy, inefficient manner. "Who did this *half-assed* job yelled the boss." 2. Stupid, lazy. "How did I ever raise such a *half-assed* son?" moaned the father."

have lead in one's ass   verb phrase. vulgar.   To be very slow-moving. (lead is a very heavy metal.) "Hurry up Joe! What's the matter, you *got lead in your ass?*" "*Get the lead out of your asses*, boys; we've got to finish this job by 5 p.m."

not know one's ass from one's elbow   verb phrase. vulgar. To be unaware, stupid, uninformed, ignorant. "How can C. be the supervisor of that company? He *doesn't know his ass from his elbow.*" Also, "He *doesn't know his ass from a hole in the ground.*"

---

a pain in the ass   noun. vulgar.   1. A very irritating person or problem. Something that is very annoying. "That neighbor is a real *pain in the ass*. She never stops complaining." "That job was a *pain in the ass*. There were many small details that had to be fixed."

piece of ass   (pēs´ ŭv ăs´)   noun. vulgar.   1. An act of sexual intercourse (*ass* here means vagina). "K. went around to all the bars looking for a *piece of ass*."   2. A woman, regarded as a sexual object only.   "'D. looks like a great *piece of ass* to me,' said E."

Shove it up your ass! Up your ass! Up yours! Angry statements. vulgar.   *It* may refer to someone's argument, apology, merchandise, gift, advice, or complaint. Also: *Stick it up your ass, Shove it*. *"You know what you can do with it"*: Euphemism for *Shove it up your ass*.

smart-ass   noun. vulgar.   1. A person who acts as if he or she knows everything; a "know-it-all."   2. A sarcastic person. Also, *wise-ass*.

tight-ass   noun. vulgar.   A person who is overly concerned with correct behavior, small details, cleanliness, and following the rules as carefully as possible. He may also be stingy, prudish, and unfriendly. "Professor T. is a real *tight-ass*. His tests are full of questions about unimportant details; no one ever gets an 'A' in his course."

You bet your sweet ass   vulgar expression.   You can be sure of it. "'Are you going to ask for your money back?' 'You bet your sweet ass I am.'"

athletic supporter   noun. euphemism.   Jockstrap. A garment worn by athletes or workers to protect the genitals from injury.

b

* **back door**   noun. slang.   The anus.

backside   noun. euphemism.   The buttocks.

* **bag**   noun. slang.   The scrotum.

* **baggie**   noun. slang.   A condom.

bald-headed hermit   noun. slang.   The penis. (A hermit is a person who lives alone. Bald = without hair on his head.)

* **ball**   verb. vulgar.   Have sexual intercourse. "They *balled* all night." "M. was *balling* N. all last summer, but no one knew about it."

ball-buster   noun. vulgar. 1. A very difficult job, boss, or person in authority who is hard to please. "The problem was a real *ball-buster*. I worked on it for eight hours and still couldn't get the right answer." "Professor B. is a real *ball-buster*. He wants students to read six chapters a week, and write three term papers." 2. A woman who makes men feel unmasculine. "Don't waste your time dating M. She'll use her charm to make you fall in love with her. Then she'll cut you in little pieces with her insults and rejection. She's a *ball-buster* all right."

* **balls**   noun. vulgar. 1. The testicles. 2. Masculine courage; nerve, daring. "That lion tamer certainly has a *lot of balls* to go into the cage with six lions." "*It takes balls* to say what you think when everyone disagrees with you." "D. was working for the company only six weeks when he asked for a ten per cent raise. *That takes balls.*"

balls, to have someone by the   verb phrase, vulgar.   To be in a position to force someone to do what is wanted. "R. wanted to divorce his wife, but she *had him by the balls*. She threatened that he'd never see the children again if he left her."

(Oh) balls!   exclamation. vulgar.   An expression of disappointment or annoyance.

ballsy   (bawl´ zē)   adjective. vulgar.   Courageous. Having masculine courage. (May be said of women, too, nowadays.)

* **bang**   verb. vulgar.   To have sexual intercourse.

bare-ass   adjective. vulgar.   Naked. Also *bared-assed*. "There was no one around, so we went swimming *bare-assed*."

bar-girl, B-girl   noun. slang.   An attractive woman who works in a bar. Her job is to encourage customers to spend more money. She behaves in a friendly, sexually inviting manner, and the customer buys drinks for her. The customer does not know that she is an employee of the bar. The bartender fills her glass with tea or colored water, and charges the price of liquor. A *bar-girl* may also sell sexual services, as a prostitute.

---

* basket   noun. slang.   1. A woman's genitals.   2. A man's genitals (homosexual use).   The shape of the man's genitals that can be seen in tight clothing.

basket days   noun, plural. slang (homosexual use).   Warm weather, when the shape of men's genitals can be seen because men are wearing light clothing such as shorts, bathing suits, running outfits, tight jeans, etc.

bastard   (băs´turd)   noun.   1. vulgar. A very disliked person.   "R. is a real *bastard*. He deserted his wife and three kids and took all of their savings, too."   2. vulgar. *Bastard* may be used in a joking way to refer to a good friend. "Mike, you old *bastard*, I haven't seen you in a long time! Where've you been?"   3. The original meaning of *bastard* is an illegitimate child; a child born to an unmarried woman. This use of the word is not vulgar.

bathroom   noun. general use.   A room with a toilet. There may also be a bathtub and a sink. The word *bathroom* used to be a euphemism. (When you go to the *bathroom* you are not really going there to take a bath!) But when a euphemism is used by everyone for a long time, its meaning becomes so clear that it no longer is a euphemism. Then a new word (such as *powder room or rest room*) is needed when one wants to avoid saying exactly what is meant.

bathroom tissue   (tĭsh´ ū)   noun. euphemism, general use.   Toilet paper. A roll of soft tissue paper used in the bathroom. The companies that make this paper label it "bathroom tissue" or "toilet tissue." Most Americans call it *toilet paper*.

* beard   (bērd)   noun. slang.   1. Female pubic hair.   2. A homosexual or straight male who accompanies a lesbian. The pair act as a couple for social purposes, but do not have a sexual relationship. "She took Joe to the convention as a *beard*."

bearded clam   (bērd ĭd klam)   noun. vulgar.   The external genitals of a woman.

beat off   verb. vulgar.   Masturbate.   "A lot of guys *beat off* after seeing a sexy movie."

beat the meat   verb phrase. vulgar.   Masturbate.

* beauts   (byūts)   noun, plural. slang.   A woman's breasts.

* beaver   (bē´ vur)   noun. vulgar.   A woman's pubic area. The vagina.

* **beaver patrol** noun phrase. vulgar expression. Looking for women, especially an opportunity to see short skirts.

bed: go to bed with verb phrase. euphemism. Have sexual intercourse with. "L. *goes to bed* with every girl he dates."

bedpan noun. general use. A special plastic or metal pan in which to urinate or defecate when one is too sick to get out of bed to go to the bathroom.

bed-wetter noun. general use. A child who continues to wet (urinate) in bed while he is sleeping although he is past 4 years old.

* **behind** euphemism. The buttocks.

belly-button noun. general use and children's word. The navel.

* **bestiality** (bēs chē ăl´ ĭ tē) noun. formal. 1. Sexual relations between a human being and some other animal. 2. Sodomy.

between the sheets noun. euphemism. Sex life. "What goes on with me and my wife *between the sheets* is none of anybody else's business."

* **bicho** (bē´ chō) noun. vulgar. Penis. (from Spanish vulgar slang)

bidet (bē dā´) noun. general use. A small washstand that a woman can sit on, and so wash the genital area easily.

birds and bees noun. euphemism. The facts about sexual reproduction. Parents who were embarrassed to speak to their children directly about human sexual activities frequently explained how flowers reproduced. Then they would progress to the reproduction of birds or other lower animals. (Father to mother), "Well, little Jimmy asked where babies come from; I guess it's time he learned about the *birds and the bees.*"

birth control noun. general use. Methods of preventing unwanted pregnancy. "If a person is going to have sexual relations, he or she should first know about *birth control.*" "What *birth control* method did your doctor recommend?"

birthday suit noun. euphemism. Naked skin. "The swimmers were wearing nothing but their *birthday suits.*"

bisexual (bī sĕk´ shū ŭl) noun. formal, general use. A person who is attracted to and can enjoy sexual relations with both males and females. Also used as an adjective. "Did you know that R. is *bisexual*? He's married and the father of two kids, but he has his boyfriends, too."

bitch (bĭ´ ch) noun. slang. 1. An unpleasant, complaining and demanding woman. 2. A sexy and attractive woman. (Original general use and formal meaning: a female dog.)

bitch verb. slang. To complain. "H. is always *bitching* about his job."

bladder (blăd´ ur) noun. formal, medical use. The organ that holds urine until it leaves the body.

blind eye noun. slang. The anus.

* **blocked up** verb phrase. euphemism. Constipated.

* **blow** (blō) verb. vulgar. Give sexual pleasure by sucking the penis orally (in the mouth). Perform fellatio.

blow a fart (blō ŭ fart´) verb phrase. vulgar. Expel gas from the rectum.

blow job noun. vulgar. Fellatio. The act of giving sexual pleasure by sucking the penis orally.

blue balls noun, plural. A mythical pain in the testicles when a man has been sexually aroused for a long time without ejaculating.

blue movies noun. slang. Pornographic movies. Movies of sexual activities.

B.O. (Bē Oh) noun. euphemism. A bad body odor, usually from the armpits.

* **bone** (bōn) noun. vulgar. The penis, when it is erect (hard).

boobs, boobies (būbz, bū´ bēz) noun plural. vulgar. Women's breasts.

booger (boo´ gur) noun. slang. A lump of dried mucus from the nose. Also, children's words: *boogie, boogieman.* There is no standard English word for this "product of nose-picking."

bordello (bor dĕl ō) noun. euphemism. House of prostitution.

bosom (boŏ´ z'm) noun. euphemism. The breast area. "The child slept with his head on his mother's *bosom*."

* **bottom** noun. euphemism. The buttocks.

bowel movement (boul´ mūv´ mĕnt) noun. formal, general use. The lower part of the digestive canal is sometimes called the bowels. To move one's bowels is to expel the waste products of digestion (feces). "The baby had a *bowel movement* in his diaper." To *move one's bowels*: = defecate. "Some doctors recommend a laxative to help you *move your bowels*."

b.m. noun. euphemism. Bowel movement. To have a *b.m.*; to make a *b.m.* (defecate).

* **box** noun. vulgar. The vagina.

box lunch noun. vulgar. Cunnilingus. Oral sex. Mouth to genital sex.

* **boy** noun. slang. Offensive when it is used by a white person to refer to a black male adult.

bra, brassiere (brŏ, brŭ zēr´) noun. general use. An article of clothing worn to give support to the breasts. "Many women do not wear a *bra* nowadays."

breast (brĕst) noun. general use. The upper chest area of either a man or a woman.

breasts (brĕsts) noun plural. general use. The mammary glands. The female organs which produce milk for a newborn baby.

* **-breasted** (brĕs tid) adjective. general use. Combined with *big*, or *small*, to described the size of the breasts. "She's a *big-breasted* woman."

breast feed verb. general use. Give a baby milk from the mother's breast. To nurse a baby. "Are you planning to *breast-feed* your baby or bottle-feed it?" "Mrs. J. *breast-fed* all seven of her children."

* **briefs** (brēfs) noun, plural. general use. Men's undershorts.

bris (brĭs) noun, religious use. The circumcision of a male Jewish baby seven days after birth. Family and friends are invited to a formal ceremony. The foreskin of the penis is cut by a special person called a merl. Then the family celebrates and has a party.

* bronx cheer (brŏnks chēr) noun. slang. A loud passing of gas from the rectum, when done on purpose to show contempt. "He lifted his leg and gave out a *Bronx cheer* to show how he felt about the offer." Also, a noise made with mouth and tongue that sounds like the passing of gas.

brothel (brŏ´ th'l) noun. formal. A house of prostitution.

* brown eye noun. slang. The anus.

* brush noun. vulgar. A woman's pubic hair.

buck snort noun. vulgar. A loud passing of intestinal gas.

* bugger (bŭg´ ur) 1. verb. vulgar. To have sexual intercourse in the rectum. Commit sodomy. 2. noun. vulgar. A person who commits buggery. A homosexual.

buggery (bŭg´ ur ē) noun. vulgar. The act of sexual intercourse in the rectum. Sodomy.

bulldyke (bŏŏl´ dīk´) noun. vulgar. (derogatory) A lesbian, particularly one who plays an aggressive role and dresses in mannish clothes.

bullshit noun. vulgar. 1. The feces of a bull (male; counterpart of cow). 2. A story or description that is not believable. Lies. "What E. told you is a *lot of bullshit*. Don't believe him." 3. Meaningless sentences, stories, or facts. "H. didn't know the answers to any of the questions on the examination, so she just wrote a whole lot of *bullshit* and hoped the professor would give her a passing grade."

bullshit verb. vulgar. 1. To tell lies or false stories. To grossly exaggerate. "Don't let P. *bullshit* you; he doesn't know what he's talking about." 2. to talk, argue, tell jokes, enjoy casual conversation among friends. "We sat around *bullshitting* until the bars closed.

* bull (bŏŏl) noun. euphemism for bullshit. "You're full of *bull*." (I don't believe you.) "Don't give me that *bull*." (Don't lie to me.) *B.S.* (be   es) = bullshit.

bullshit artist noun. vulgar. A person who tells incredible stories and succeeds in convincing other people that the stories are true. "G. would make a good salesman. He's quite a *bullshit artist*."

* **bumpers** noun, plural. slang. A woman's breasts. (The reference is to the bumpers on cars that cushion the impact with another car.)

bung hole noun. vulgar. The anus.

* **buns** noun. plural. slang euphemism. The buttocks. "He has a nice pair of *buns*."

bunny noun. slang. A loose woman. A male or female prostitute.

bunnyfuck verb. vulgar. Very rapid intercourse.

* **bush** (bŏŏsh) noun. vulgar. A woman's pubic hair.

* **bust** (bŭst) noun. general use. The breast area of a woman. This word is used in giving the measurements of the body and for clothing sizes. "Miss America has a *36-inch bust*, a 25-inch waist, and 38-inch hips." "Blouses, brassieres, and bathing suits are generally marked with the *bust* size."

* **butch** (bŏŏch) noun. slang. A female homosexual who is masculine in appearance, dress, or manner.

* **butt** (bŭt) noun. slang. The buttocks. "G. is lazy. He needs a good kick in the *butt* to get him to do a job."

buttocks (bŭt´ ŭks) noun. formal, general use. The fatty, muscular area of the lower back.

button noun. slang. The clitoris. Also, *love button*.

C

* **caboose** (kă būs´) noun. slang. The buttocks. (A caboose is the last car on a train.) "Look at the *caboose* on that fat lady, will ya?"

call girl noun. general use. A high-priced prostitute who works by telephone appointment and not in a house of prostitution or on the street.

* **can** noun. slang. 1. The buttocks. "He fell on his *can*." 2. The bathroom. "Who's in the *can*? Hurry up! I have to go, too!"

carnal knowledge (kar´ nŭl nŏl´ ĕj) noun phrase. euphemism. Sexual intimacy.

---

castrate (kăs´ trāt´) verb. formal, medical use. Remove the testicles by surgery (synonyms: neuter, fix). This is usually done on male cattle for the purpose of great and faster growth. "Bulls are *castrated* so they will be easier to handle and the meat will be more tender." A *castrated* bull is called a steer. "Male cats are often *castrated* to prevent their habit of urinating on furniture."

cathouse noun. slang. A house of prostitution.

cervix (sur´ vĭks) noun. medical use. The neck or opening of the uterus.

change of life noun. euphemism. The menopause in women. A woman's ability to have children stops when she is between ages 40 and 55. She stops menstruating and her ovaries stop producing estrogen (a female hormone). Sometimes this causes nervous symptons and physical discomfort. "My wife is going through the *change of life*. She is frequently upset for no apparent reason." Also, *the change*.

* **cheap** adjective. derogatory slang used by women about a woman. Having low morals, dressing in poor taste, wearing too much makeup, easy for men to have sexual relations with. "Look at that blonde. With all that makeup and the low-cut blouse, she sure looks *cheap*."

* **cheat** 1. verb. slang. To be unfaithful to one's husband, wife, or steady sex partner. To have sexual relations with another person without the knowledge of one's usual partner. To commit adultery. "M. *cheats* on her husband all the time." "Y. never *cheats* on his girlfriend." 2. noun. slang. A person who is not faithful to a lover or spouse (spouse = a husband or wife).

check the plumbing verb phrase. male euphemism. Go to the bathroom. "Excuse me. I'll be back as soon as I *check the plumbing*." Also, *inspect the plumbing*.

* **cheeks** noun, plural. general use. The two round fatty sections of the buttocks. Sometimes called the "lower cheeks" to distinguish from cheeks on the face.

* **cherry** noun. vulgar. The hymen. The flap of skin that covers part of the vagina before a woman's first act of sexual intercourse. An unbroken hymen is considered to be a sign of virginity.

to still have a cherry vulgar. To be a virgin (a woman who has never had sexual intercourse).

to lose one's cherry   vulgar.   To have intercourse for the first time, losing one's virginity.

to bust a cherry   vulgar.   To have sexual intercourse with a girl who is a virgin.

* **chest**   noun.   1. general use.   The front area of the body between the shoulders and the waist on either a man or a woman.   2. slang.   The breasts of a woman.

* **chicken**   noun.   slang.   A young male prostitute who sells sexual services to older male homosexuals.

* **chicken hawk**   noun.   slang.   A male homosexual who buys the sexual services of a young male prostitute.

chicken shit   noun.   vulgar.   Something that is completely worthless, uninteresting, and unrewarding.   Also used as an adjective.   "Y. said he hated his *chicken shit* job so he was planning to quit."

chocha   (chō´ chū)   noun.   vulgar.   Vagina (from Spanish).

choke the chicken   verb phrase.   vulgar.   Masturbate.

circumcision   (sur´ kŭm sĭ´ zhun)   noun.   formal, general use.   A surgical procedure to remove part of the foreskin of a baby boy's penis.   It is done for religious reasons or health reasons.   "All Jewish baby boys are *circumcised* (sur kum sizd) seven days after birth."   The formal ceremony to which family and friends are invited is called a *bris*.

clap, the   (klăp)   noun.   vulgar.   Gonorrhea, a venereal disease.   A disease that is gotten through sexual contact with an infected person.   "R. *got the clap* from a 42nd Street prostitute."

* **climax**   (klī´ măks)   noun.   formal, general use.   Orgasm. The moment of most intense pleasure during sexual intercourse. The male *climax* is when he ejaculates.   A woman's *climax* is when there are rhythmic contractions in the vagina.   "A man may reach *climax* before his partner."   verb use also.   "They *climax*ed together."

clitoris   (klī´ tūr ĭs)   noun.   formal, medical, general use. The small, highly sensitive organ that is located in the forward part of the vulva.   This is the organ in the female that is responsible for much sexual pleasure and orgasm.   adjective form: clitoral.

---

clit (klĭt)　noun.　slang.　The clitoris.

closet queen　noun.　slang.　A male homosexual who does not act like a homosexual in public. His neighbors and co-workers may think he is heterosexual.

　to come out of the closet　verb phrase.　slang.　To stop hiding one's homosexuality. Stop pretending in public to be a heterosexual. "When the Gay Liberation Movement began, thousands of gay men and women *came out of the closet*."

* **coconuts**　(kō′ kŭ nŭts)　noun.　plural.　A woman's breasts.

* **cock**　(kŏk)　noun.　1. vulgar.　The penis. This is one of the most common terms used among men to refer to the male sex organ. 2. general use.　A rooster (male chicken).

* **cockpit**　(kŏk′ pĭt)　noun.　vulgar.　A woman's genitals.

cock sucker　noun.　vulgar.　Literally, a person who sucks cock (performs fellatio); a male homosexual. The word is more often used as an insult to describe a hateful person. It is similar to, but much stronger than the words *bastard* and *son of a bitch*.

cock tease　(kŏk′ tēz′)　noun.　vulgar.　A woman who acts as though she were sexually interested in a man, but who will not have intercourse with him after he has become aroused. "J. has the reputation of being a *cock tease*."

cohabit　(kō hǎ′ bĭt)　verb.　formal, legal.　1. To live together as man and wife, even though unmarried. 2. To have regular sexual relations when married. "Mr. C. wanted a divorce on the grounds that his wife refused to *cohabit* with him."

coitus　(kō′ ĭ tŭs)　noun.　formal, medical use.　Sexual intercourse. "During *coitus*, the blood pressure and pulse of both partners rises." "The average married couple in their twenties *engage in coitus* three to five times a week."

cojones, also cohones　(kō hō′ nāz)　noun, plural. vulgar.　1. Testicles. "Look at the *cojones* on that dog!" 2. Masculine courage. "It takes *cojones* to be in the Marines."

colorful language　noun.　general use and euphemism. Speech that is full of slang or vulgar expressions, or unusual ways of describing things. "Reading this book will help you to understand some *colorful language*."

* **come** 1. verb. slang. Have an orgasm or sexual climax (in a male, ejaculate). "J. always *comes* three or four times before K. *comes*." "Did you *come* yet?" (A common question by anxious lovers.) "'I'm c-c-c-*coming*!' she moaned." 2. noun. slang. The semen that is ejaculated during orgasm.

* **come across** verb phrase. slang. To submit to a man's sexual advances. "Women don't *come across* easily anymore. I guess they're all afraid of getting AIDS."

comfort station (kŭm´ furt stā´ shŭn) noun. euphemism. A public bathroom, usually along a well-traveled highway.

commode (kŭ mōd´) noun. euphemism. A toilet.

* **conceive** (kŭn sēv´) verb. formal, general use. To become pregnant. "H. has been trying to *conceive* ever since she got married."

* **conception** (kŭn sĕp´ shŭn) noun. formal, medical use. The union of the male sex cell (sperm) with the female sex cell (ova). "New life begins at the moment of *conception*."

condom (kŏn´ dŭm) noun. general use. A contraceptive worn by the male on the penis. It may be made of very thin rubber or the thin membrane of animal intestines. "The *condom* is 94% safe as a preventative of pregnancy."

constipated (kŏn´ stĭ pā´ tĭd) adjective. formal, general use. Unable to defecate; having difficulty in passing stool. "Everytime A. ate cheese, she became *constipated*, and didn't have a bowel movement for days."

constipation (kŏn´ stĭ pā´ shĭn) noun. formal and general use. Difficulty in moving one's bowels. "To avoid *constipation*, eat salads, raw fruits, and whole grains. Drink plenty of water."

contraception (kŏn trŭ sĕp´ shin) noun. formal, general use. Methods of preventing pregnancy. Birth control. "J. asked her doctor if there were any new forms of *contraception* that were more effective than "the pill.""

* **coolie** (kū´ lē) noun. children's word, euphemism. The buttocks.

copulate (kŏp yū lāt´) verb. formal, medical use. Have sexual intercourse. "Most animals *copulate* less frequently than human beings."

---

* crabs noun, plural. general use. A certain kind of lice that live in the pubic hair of humans. They are very tiny and extremely itchy. "*Crabs* can be caught from close personal contact, from bedsheets, or from sitting on a toilet that has been used by someone with *crabs*."

crab ladder noun. slang, humorous use. Some men have hair leading from the pubic area to the navel. This hair could supposedly be used by crabs (lice-if the person had them) to climb to the midsection of the body.

* crack noun. vulgar. The vagina.

* cramps (krămps) noun, plural. general use. Contractions of the intestine or uterus that cause pain. "C. always *gets cramps* on the first day of her menstrual period."

* crap noun. 1. vulgar. Feces (synonym: shit).

take a crap verb. vulgar. Defecate.

full of crap adjective. vulgar. Full of lies and unbelievable stories. "J. is *full of crap*. Don't follow his advice, whatever you do." 2. Worthless things. "Why did you buy all that *crap*? You've wasted a lot of your money." "K. ate lots of *crap*" (such as candy, soda, chocolate, beer, potato chips).

* cream 1. noun. vulgar. Semen. 2. verb. vulgar. To ejaculate, to have an orgasm.

To cream in one's jeans verb expression. vulgar. Literally, to ejaculate with one's pants still on. This is often an exaggerated way of saying that someone is very sexually aroused. "P. nearly *creamed in his jeans* when the actress walked into the room."

crotch (krŏch) noun. general use. The pubic area. The angle formed by the two legs where they join the body. (A tree has a crotch, too.)

crotch rot (krŏch′ rŏt′) noun. slang. Itchy, irritable skin in the crotch area.

crud (krŭd) noun. slang. 1. Dried semen. 2. any disgusting dirt or dried food.

* cucumber (kyū′ kŭm bŭr) noun. 1. slang. The penis. 2. slang. An artificial penis, or a device to use for masturbation.

cunnilingus (kŭn´ ĭ lĭn gŭs) noun. formal. Oral-genital contact. Stimulation of the female genitalia by the partner's tongue.

cuckold (kŭ´ kld) 1. noun. slang. A husband whose wife has been unfaithful. 2. verb. slang. To make one's husband a cuckold by having sex with another man.

cunt (kŭnt) noun. vulgar. 1. The vagina. 2. A woman (derogatory).

curse (kurs) verb. general use. 1. To use vulgar language. To swear. "R. was so angry he *cursed* for five minutes." 2. To ask God or the Devil to cause bad luck or injury to happen to someone or something. "We *cursed* the landlord for raising the rent." 3. noun. general use. Any vulgar word. "M. knows a lot of *curses* and he's only five years old." Bad luck sent by God or the Devil or one's enemies. "D. blamed all of his bad luck on a *curse* that his enemies had put on him."

curse, the noun. slang. The menstrual period. "H. won't go swimming because she has *the curse*." (This word implies that the speaker has a negative feeling about this natural body function.)

* **cut the cheese** verb phrase. slang. To expel gas from the rectum. "Phew, what a smell! Who *cut the cheese*?"

cut a fart verb. vulgar. To expel gas from the rectum. Also: *cut one*. "Y. ate rice and beans for lunch and he's been *cutting farts* all afternoon."

d

damn! damn it! (dăm, dăm ĭt) interjection. vulgar. An expression of anger or disappointment. *God damn it!* vulgar. Expression of extreme irritation or anger. "*Damn* you! I told you not to bother me when I'm busy!" (The verb *damn* means to condemn to Hell or eternal punishment after death. Technically, the word is not vulgar, but Christian church teachings forbid the use of this word as an expression of anger.)

damned, damn (dămd, dăm) adjective. vulgar. Annoying, broken, useless, worthless. "This *damn* car isn't any *damn* good!" "You *damn* idiot! You've ruined everything.!"

* **dark meat** vulgar expression. Sex with a black woman. "H. says he likes a little *dark meat* now and then."

darn, darn it! interjections. slang, euphemisms for damn and damn it.

date rape expression. slang. Forcible sexual intercourse while on a date. This is a crime.

* **deceive (one's husband or wife)** (de sev) verb. general use (now considered old-fashioned). To have sexual relations with a partner different from one's own husband or wife.

defecate (dĕ´ fŭ kāt) verb. formal. To expel (push out) feces from the rectum.

delicate parts of the anatomy noun phrase, plural. euphemism. Genitals, usually male testicles. "Women, if you are attacked by a rapist, try to kick him in the *delicate parts of his anatomy.*"

derriere (der´ ē ār) noun. euphemism. Buttocks. This is borrowed from the French.

* **desire** (dē zīr´) 1. verb. general use. To want in a sexual way. To have a sexual need for someone. 2. noun. A sexual need. "His *desire* for her increased each day that she rejected him."

* **diaphragm** (dī´ ŭ frăm) noun. formal, general use. 1. A contraceptive device. It is a circle of rubber that is inserted into the woman's vagina before intercourse and prevents sperm from entering the uterus. 2. There are many other nonsexual uses of the word *diaphragm*, in the fields of anatomy, electronics, optics, and mechanics.

diarrhea (dī´ ŭ rē´ ŭ) noun. formal, general use. Frequent need to defecate. The feces are watery and hard to control. "L. had *diarrhea* from eating green apples." "The druggist said to *take Kaopectate®* to stop *diarrhea.*"

* **dick** noun. vulgar. The penis.

diddle (dĭd´ ul) verb. vulgar. 1. To masturbate. 2. To have sexual intercourse. 3. To waste time. "Stop *diddling* around and get to work!" 4. To cheat someone.

dildo (dĭl´ dō) noun. vulgar. 1. An artificial penis used for masturbation or sexual play. 2. An extremely stupid or clumsy person.

dingle berry (dĭn´ gul ber´ ē) noun. vulgar. 1. A small piece of feces caught in the crotch hairs near the anus. 2. A stupid person.

* **dipstick** (dĭp´ stĭk) noun. vulgar. Penis. (A dipstick is a long measuring tool stored in a car's engine to check the oil.)

* **dirty** adjective. slang. Having a vulgar or sexual meaning: dirty words, dirty pictures, dirty jokes, dirty movies, etc.

  to have a dirty mind slang. To think of sex often. To think that other people are always thinking of sex. To interpret words with double meanings in their sexual meanings rather than in their general use meanings.

  dirty old man noun. slang. An older man who is interested in flirting, touching, and seducing women. This may be used either as a term of affection or in a derogatory way.

* **discharge** (dĭs´ charj) noun. formal, general use. A liquid that comes out of the penis or vagina indicating that there is an infection or diseased condition. "She went to the gynecologist for a checkup because she had a frequent bad-smelling *discharge*." "One symptom of gonorrhea is a pus-like *discharge* from the penis."

* **diving suit** (dī´ ving sūt) noun. slang. Condom.

* **do it** verb. slang. To have sexual intercourse.

  dog style (dawg stīl) adverb. slang. Sexual intercourse with the woman on her hands and knees, and the man entering the vagina from the rear.

* **doodle** noun. vulgar. Penis.

  doo doo (dū dū) noun. children's word. Feces. Also, *doodee. make doo doo* verb. Defecate.

  dork (dork) noun. vulgar. Penis.

  double meaning noun. general use. Having two meanings, one of which is vulgar or sexual. "Words with *double meanings* are often the basis of jokes."

  douche (dūsh) verb. formal. To clean the vagina with water or medicated fluid, using a douche bag and syringe. "The doctor advised her to *douche* twice a week for four weeks." *Warning: This word does not mean "shower."* The Spanish word "ducha," French "douche," and other European words look similar, but the meaning is *not* the same.

---

douche bag (dūsh bă g) 1. noun. general use. The bag that contains the water for the douche. 2. vulgar. A very stupid, disliked person.

down: to go down on verb. vulgar. To perform fellatio or cunnilingus. To give mouth-to-genital stimulation.

down there noun. euphemism. The pubic area. The genitals. "J. fell of his bicycle and hurt himself, uh, you know...*down there.*"

* **drag** noun. slang. A male who is wearing woman's clothing is said to be *"in drag."*

drain a lizard (drān ŭ lĭz´urd) verb phrase. slang. Urinate.

drain a vein (drān ŭ vān) verb phrase. slang. Urinate.

* **drawers** (drorz) noun. general use. Undershorts or panties.

drop one's load verb. vulgar. To ejaculate.

dry hump (drĭ hŭmp) verb. vulgar. To go through the motions of sexual intercourse completely clothed and without any actual genital contact.

duff (dŭf) noun. euphemism. The buttocks. *"On one's duff"* means "sitting." "Get off your duff and let's get going."

* **dump, dump a load** (dŭmp ŭ lōd) verb phrase. vulgar. Defecate.

* **duster** noun. slang. euphemism. The buttocks.

dyke (dĭk) noun. slang. A lesbian (female homosexual) who plays a masculine role. She may dress in mannish clothing and walk, talk, and act in a masculine manner.

diesel dyke (dēz'l dĭk) a large, very aggressive lesbian.

dysmenorrhea (dĭs mĕn´ or rē´ ŭ) noun. formal. Medical use. Painful cramps that accompany the menstrual period. "Some teenagers suffer from *dysmenorrhea*, but it is less common among mature women."

e

easy make noun. slang (derogatory). A woman who will consent to have sexual intercourse with a man whom she doesn't know very well.

* **eat, eat it raw**   verb. vulgar.   To perform cunnilingus or fellatio. To stimulate the genitals of one's partner with the mouth and tongue.

* **egg**   (ĕg)   noun. general use.   The ovum, or female sex cell.

* **ejaculate**   (ē jăk´ yū lāt)   1. verb. formal.   To eject semen at the time of climax (male). 2. noun. formal.   Semen.

* **eliminate**   (ē lĭm ĭn āt)   verb. formal.   To excrete waste products. Technically this word includes perspiration, urination and defecation. It is often used, however, in the sense of defecation alone.

empty one's bladder   verb phrase. formal.   To urinate. (Nurse to patient) "The doctor would like you to *empty your bladder* before the examination."

enema   (ĕ´ nŭ mŭ)   noun. general use.   A cleaning out of the rectum and lower colon by injecting warm water through the anus. "T. was constipated; the doctor advised him to take an *enema*." "The nurse gave the patient an *enema* before the operation."

enuresis   (ēn yū rē´ sĭs)   noun. formal. Medical use. 1. A problem of urinating in bed while one is asleep. "D. suffered from *enuresis* until he was eleven years old."   2. Loss of control of the bladder. "Many elderly people begin to suffer from *enuresis*."

* **equipment**   (ē kwĭp mĕnt)   noun. slang.   Male sex organs.

    The right equipment   slang.   Attractive shape, for a female (said by a male, as a compliment).

* **erect, to be**   (tū bē ē rĕkt´)   verb phrase. general use. When the penis is firm, engorged with blood and ready for sexual intercourse.

an erection   (ē rĕk´ shŭn)   noun. general use.   A firm or erect penis. "E. gets an *erection* whenever he sees C." "T. *lost his erection* when he heard the baby cry."

erotic   (er ŏ´ tĭk)   adjective. general use.   Sexually stimulating. "K. likes *erotic* stories and movies."

erotica   (ĕ rŏt´ ĭ kŭ)   noun, plural.   Collections of pictures and stories referring to sex.

---

* **escort service** (ĕs´ kort sur´ vĭs) noun. euphemism.
Male companion, who will escort a woman to dinner or parties,
for a fee. He may or may not also provide sex.

eunuch (yū´ nĭk) noun. formal, general use. A male
whose testicles have been removed in childhood, or whose
testicles do not function normally. A *eunuch* does not have a
deep masculine voice, beard, or pubic hair and cannot have
sexual intercourse.

* **excited** adjective. general use. 1. Aroused emotionally.
"The child was *excited* on his birthday." 2. Aroused sexually.

* **exhibitionist** (ĕk´ sĭ bĭ´ shŭn ĭst) noun. general use.
1. A person who acts in a way to attract attention to himself.
Actors, politicians, and other performers are exhibitionists in a
way. 2. A person who receives sexual pleasure from showing
parts of his or her body in public to strangers.

* **expect** verb. general use. To wait for the birth of a baby.
To be pregnant. "J. is *expecting* in July (she will give birth to a
baby in July)."

expectant (ĕks pĕk´ tĕnt) adjective. general use.
Pregnant. "Mrs. T went to a clinic for *expectant* mothers."
"When are you expecting? (common question asked of pregnant
women.) "The Johnsons are *expecting* a visit from the stork."
(A stork is a long-billed bird. Traditionally, parents did not
feel comfortable in discussing reproduction with children and so
told them the story that babies are "brought by the stork.")

f

F (ĕf) verb. vulgar, euphemism. Abbreviation of *fuck*.
"'F you!' she shouted." "Get the F out of here!" "Where's the
F-ing key?"

* **facilities, the** (fŭ sĭl´ ĭ tēz) noun, plural. slang. The
bathroom. "Excuse me, may I *use your facilities*?"

facts of life, the noun phrase. euphemism. The facts
about sex and reproduction. "H. thought his son was old
enough to learn *the facts of life*. It was too late. He had
learned them from his best friend when he was six years old."

fag, faggot (făg, făg´ ĭt) noun. slang. (derogatory)
A male homosexual.

* **fairy**　(fār´ē)　noun. slang.　A homosexual.

* **faithful**　(fāth´fŭl)　adjective. general use, euphemism. Having sexual intercourse with one partner only. "M.'s husband has always been *faithful* to her, and she has been a *faithful* wife."

　　unfaithful　(ŭn fāth´fŭl)　adjective. euphemism.　The opposite of *faithful*. "When G. found out her husband had been *unfaithful*, she decided to ask for a divorce."

fake an orgasm, fake it　(fāk´ ăn or´ găzm)　verb phrase. slang.　To pretend to reach a sexual climax by dramatically acting as if one were receiving intense pleasure. "K. *faked orgasm* just to please her husband."

falsies　(fawl´sēz)　noun, plural. slang.　Rubber or cotton pads placed in a woman's brassiere to give the appearance of having larger breasts. "Nobody knew she wore *falsies*."

family jewels, the　(thŭ făm´lē jūlz)　noun, plural. slang, humorous.　The male sex organs, penis and testicles. Sometimes just the testicles. (Jewels are precious stones such as rubies and diamonds. This expression shows a high regard placed on the male sex organs.)

fanny　(făn´ē)　noun. slang.　The buttocks.

fart　(fart)　1. verb. vulgar.　Expel gas from the rectum. "Beans make you *fart*." "L. *farted* and blamed it on the dog." 2. noun. vulgar.　The gas that is expelled.

　　lay a fart, blow a fart, let loose a fart, give out a fart vulgar.　Expel gas.

feces　(fē´sēz)　noun, plural. formal, medical use.　The undigestible waste that is expelled from the rectum when one goes to the toilet.

fellatio　(fĕl ā´shō)　noun. formal.　Oral-genital contact. Mouth to penis sexual stimulation.

　　to perform fellatio　formal.　To give sexual pleasure by stimulating the penis with the mouth.

feminine syringe　(fĕm´ĭn ĭn sĭ rĭnj´)　noun. euphemism.　A douche bag and hose for cleaning the vagina.

---

fetishist (fĕt´ ĭsh ĭst) noun. formal. A person who becomes sexually aroused by a particular part of a woman, her clothing, or some object. "She has a hair *fetish*, and he was a foot *fetishist*; with her big feet, and his mop of hair, they got along very well."

* **finger** 1. noun. slang. *To give the finger* is to make an obscene gesture, with the middle finger extended and the other fingers folded down. It translates: "Stick this up your ass." 2. verb. slang. To stimulate a woman's genitals with the fingers. *Finger fuck* = to masturbate a woman using one's fingers.

* **flasher** (flăsh´ ur) noun. slang. A man who gets sexually aroused by showing his penis to strange women in public. He may wear a raincoat covering his unzipped pants, and *flash* his coat open when a woman alone approaches him.

flog one's dong (flŏg´ wŭnz dŏng) verb phrase. vulgar. Masturbate.

* **fly** noun. general use. The zipper or buttons in the front of trousers or pants. "J. was embarrassed to discover that his *fly* was open. He quickly zipped up his *fly*."

* **foreplay** (for´ plā) noun. general use. Sexual play before intercourse. Includes touching, kissing, talking, massaging, etc. "D. wanted her husband to pay more attention to *foreplay* when he made love to her."

fornicate (for´ nĭ kāt) verb. formal, legal use; derogatory general use. To have sexual intercourse with someone that one is not married to. "*Fornication* is against the law in many states."

foul language (foul lăn´ gwĭj) noun. general use. Vulgar language. "'We don't want any *foul language* in this playground,' said the police officer."

foul mouth noun. general use. A person who uses vulgar words frequently in places where it is socially unacceptable. "My friend G. has a *foul mouth*; I'm embarrassed to go to parties with her."

four-letter words noun, plural. general use. Vulgar words. Many vulgar words contain just four letters, such as piss, shit, fart, fuck, cock, cunt, hell, damn.

* **fox,** also, *foxy lady* noun. slang. A sexually attractive, clever, independent and fashionable woman.

free love noun. euphemism. Sexual relationships without marriage. "'The younger generation all believe in *free love,'* complained the old lady."

* **french** verb. slang. To perform fellatio or cunnilingus. Oral stimulation of the genitals.

French kiss noun. slang. Kissing in which the tongue is inserted in the partner's mouth.

French letter noun. slang. A condom.

* **friend, my** noun. euphemism. The menstrual period. "I can't go swimming because I've got *my friend.*"

frig (frĭg) vulgar. verb. euphemism for *fuck.* Generally used in expressions that do not imply sexual intercourse.

'friggin' (frĭg´ĭn) adjective. Less offensive form of *fucking.*

* **frigid** (frĭ´jĭd) adjective. general use. 1. Cold. 2. Unable to respond sexually (said of a woman). Unable to have orgasm. "It is as miserable to *be* a *frigid* wife as it is to *have* a *frigid* wife."

frigidity (frĭ´jĭ´dĭ tē) noun. general use. Inability to respond sexually. "C. went to a sex therapy clinic to see if her *frigidity* could be cured."

* **fruit** noun. slang (derogatory). Homosexual.

fuck (fŭk) verb. vulgar. 1. To have sexual intercourse (with). This is the most common vulgar word for sexual intercourse. (There is *no* simple general use verb for this act!) The word *fuck* also has many other meanings that have no relationship with sexual activity. *They are all considered vulgar, however.* 2. To treat badly or unfairly; to cheat. "Don't deal with that company; they *fuck* all their customers." "J. got *fucked*" by his business partners and lost all his money." 3. The word *fuck* can be added in the middle of a command to add emphasis or show anger: "Shut *the fuck* up!" Sit *the fuck* down." It can be added to questions with the same effect: "*Who the fuck* is that?" "*Where the fuck* are we?" "*Why the fuck* didn't you tell me?" "*What the fuck* are you doing?"

fuck up (fŭk´ ŭp´) 1. verb. vulgar. Do an incompetent job, creating more work for others. Ruin; confuse; make serious errors. "The hospital really *fucked up* this bill." "The architect *fucked up* the design of this house. He didn't leave enough room for the upstairs stairway." 2. noun. vulgar. An incompetent person. Someone who usually makes things worse when he does a job. "D. is a real *fuck up*. No matter how many times you explain something to him, he manages to do it wrong."

fuck someone up verb. vulgar. Cause someone to suffer mental or physical injury. To confuse. "The Army really *fucked up* J.'s mind."

fuck around verb. vulgar. 1. Fool around. Annoy. "Stop *fucking around*! I'm getting angry." 2. Be idle; loiter at a place without any purposeful activity. "We went down to the ball field and just *fucked around* for awhile; there wasn't anything else to do."

fuck with verb. vulgar. Interfere with; touch with intention of hurting or damaging; deal with in a dishonest way. "Anyone who *fucks with* old Sam better be careful. Sam'll kill him."

fuck one's fist verb phrase. vulgar. Masturbate.

fuck one's mind verb. vulgar. Brain wash. To confuse permanently. "E. joined the Z. gang and they really *fucked his mind*; he won't even talk to his own mother anymore."

fuck you! interjection. vulgar. 1. Damn you! Said in great anger with hopes that the listener will have serious bad luck. 2. No. Leave me alone. You irritate me.

(Go) fuck yourself vulgar. Interjection showing great anger and contempt for the listener.

I don't give a fuck vulgar. I don't care in the least. It's completely unimportant to me. "*I don't give a fuck* what you say; I'm going to do this *my* way."

fucking adjective. vulgar. 1. Bad, rotten, no-good, worthless. "P. is a *fucking* idiot." 2. Among some groups of men, such as sailors, soldiers, prisoners, the word *fucking* is used by habit as an adjective in front of any noun. "Pass the *fucking* salt." "Where's the *fucking* knife?" It has no meaning, other than to establish the manhood of the speaker, or the bond among men of a similar social class. 3. adverb. Very. "That's *fucking* great!" It is also used in these groups as an internal part of a larger word into which it is inserted, like a sandwich. Absolutely becomes *abso-fucking-lutely*. Unconscious becomes *un-fucking-conscious*. Irresponsible becomes *irre-fucking-sponsible*.

fucker noun. vulgar. Disliked person. "X? Oh, that *fucker*? Don't trust him."

    mother-fucker noun. vulgar. 1. A hateful person. "You rotten *mother-fucker*! Get the hell out of here!" 2. A good friend. "M., you old *mother-fucker*! It's good to see you!"

    m.f. vulgar. euphemism for *mother-fucker*

full of it; full of shit; full of bull; full of crap vulgar. Full of lies and exaggerated stories. "Don't listen to J. He's *full of it*."

full of piss and vinegar phrase. vulgar. Energetic, vigorous, outspoken. "My grandfather was ninety years old, but he was still *full of piss and vinegar*, and often did and said things that shocked us younger kids."

* **fundament** (fŭn´ dŭ mĭnt) noun. slang. The buttocks.

furburger (fur´ bur gur) noun. vulgar. The vulva. The entrance to the vagina.

g

G-spot noun. slang. A small area in the front wall of the vagina that, when stimulated during intercourse or masturbation may cause female ejaculation, and a great release of body tension.

gang bang noun. vulgar. A party where several males take turns having intercourse with one female.

---

* **gas**   noun. general use.   Intestinal gas. "Doctor, I get *gas* when I eat cabbage."

   pass gas   (pas gas)   verb. general use.   Expel gas from the rectum.

* **gay**   (gā)   adjective. slang.   Homosexual, either male or female. This word is preferred by homosexuals. It is non-derogatory. In the past few years, Americans have stopped using the word *gay* in its former meaning of "happy, jolly, care-free," in order to avoid misunderstanding. An older person might still say, "It was a *gay* party." However, to most Americans, this sentence now means, "It was a party for homosexuals," and not, "It was a jolly party."

   Gay Rights Movement   noun. general use.   Organized campaigns, demonstrations, and activities to increase the rights of homosexuals. Also referred to as *Gay Liberation*. Some of the goals are: change laws that discriminate against homosexuals; equal rights in employment, housing, health care, and child custody laws.

   gender   (jĕn´ dur)   noun. general use.   There are three genders: masculine (male), feminine (female), and neuter (neither male nor female). "What *gender* are the puppies?" "They're male." "We had our male cat neutered."

   genitalia   (jĕn´ ĭ tāl´ ya)   noun, plural. formal.   Sex organs. Reproductive organs of male or female. "The penis, testicles, vagina, and vulva are all part of human *genitalia*."

* **get hot**   verb phrase. slang.   Become sexually excited.

   get into her pants   verb phrase. vulgar.   Have intercourse with a woman. "V. wanted to *get into his girlfriend's pants*, but she wanted to wait until she knew him better."

   get one's end wet   verb phrase. vulgar.   Be successful at seducing a woman. "Did you *get your end wet* last night?"

   get it up   verb phrase. slang.   Have an erection. "J. really wanted to have intercourse that night, but he was too tired to *get it up*."

   get a little action   noun. slang.   Sexual activity. "The sailors visited a bar to see if they could *get a little action* with the women there."

get one's shit together   verb phrase. vulgar.   To get organized; become prepared. "It's just a few days before the inspectors come, and this place is a mess. *We've got to get our shit together*, and straighten up."

G.I.B.   (jē ī bē)   adjective. slang.   G ood *I* n *B* ed. Passionate. Sexually responsive and fun. Having the qualities of a good sex partner.

gigolo   (jĭ´ gŭ lō)   noun. general use.   A young man who has a relationship with a woman (usually older, or richer). He is not paid as a prostitute, but may receive money, gifts, presents, favors, or complete support as tokens of appreciation for his attention.

give head   verb phrase. vulgar.   Perform fellatio, or cunnilingus. Give mouth to genital stimulation.

give a shot   verb phrase. vulgar.   Ejaculate in a woman.

gluteus maximus   (glū tē ŭs măks´ ŭ mŭs)   noun. formal, medical use.   The buttocks. The word is used humorously also, "Get off your *gluteus maximus* and start to work."

* **go**   (gō)   verb. euphemism.   Abbreviated form of *go to the toilet*. "Hurry up there in the bathroom. I have to *go!*"

gonads   (gō´ nădz)   noun, plural. formal, medical use. The reproductive organs, the testes and the ovaries. Sex glands.

gonorrhea   (gŏ´ nur ē ŭ)   noun. formal, medical use. A disease that affects the sex organs. It is given to another person through sexual contact. One of the venereal diseases. Symptoms in the man are a pus-filled discharge from the penis and painful urination. A woman may have *gonorrhea* with no visible external symptoms.

goose   (gūs)   verb. slang.   Insert (or try to insert) a finger into another person's anus. This may be done as a joke or playful teasing.

go up the old dirt road   verb phrase. slang.   Anal intercourse.

Greek way, the   adverbial phrase. slang.   Anal intercourse.

groin   (groin)   noun. general use.   The crotch area. The pubic area. "The football player pulled a muscle in his *groin*."

---

gynecologist (gī´nŭ kŏl ŭ jĭst) noun. formal. A doctor who specializes in treating women's reproductive system concerns. A *gynecologist* may also be an *obstetrician*.

obstetrician (ŏb stŭ trĭ´shŭn) (a specialist in delivering babies).

h

hair pie noun. vulgar. The female genitalia, especially when considered as the object of cunnilingus, or mouth-to-genital stimulation.

half-assed adjective. vulgar. Stupid, lazy.

* **hams** noun, plural. slang. The buttocks.

* **hammer** noun. vulgar. The penis. "How's your *hammer* hanging?" (A greeting among college males.)

hand job noun phrase. slang. Masturbation by hand.

hard-on noun. vulgar. An erection (of the penis). "G. wakes up every morning with a *hard-on*."

harlot (har´lŭt) noun. slang. A cheap prostitute.

* **head** noun. 1. slang. The bathroom. This term is most common among sailors, but is also used in bars and taverns. 2. general use. The head of the penis.

to give head verb phrase. vulgar. To perform fellatio or cunnilingus on one's partner. To orally stimulate the genitals.

* **headache, to have a** verb phrase. euphemism. Often said by women when they are not interested in having sex at the moment. "Not tonight, honey, *I've got a headache*," is now a standard joke.

* **headlights** noun, plural. A woman's breasts, especially large ones.

* **heat, bitch in** noun. vulgar. A sexually agressive woman.

* **heinie** (hī´nē) noun. children's word. The buttocks.

Hell   noun. general use, but restricted by Christian church teachings. *Hell* is a place where the souls or spirits of dead people go if they had been bad during their life on earth (according to traditional Christian teachings). In Hell, the souls are punished by fire and by devils. The opposite of Heaven.

Go to Hell   (gō tū hĕl)   Interjection of annoyance at someone.   The words *the hell* are inserted to add emphasis and anger to the questions that follow.   *"Why the hell* did you do that?"   *"What the hell* do you think you're doing?"   *"Where the hell* are you going."   *"Who the hell* do you think you are?"

* **hemispheres**   (hĕm´ ĭs fērz)   noun, plural. slang.   A woman's breasts.

hemorrhoids   (hĕm´ ur oidz)   noun. formal, general use. Painful enlargements of veins near the anus. Piles. "His doctor told him that chronic constipation can cause *hemorrhoids*."

hermaphrodite   (hur mă´ frĭ dĭt)   noun. formal.   An abnormal person who has both male and female sex organs.

herpes   (hur´ pēz)   noun. formal, general use.   There are two kinds: oral (on the mouth) herpes and genital herpes. It is a virus that causes painful blisters. It can be transmitted through kissing, sex, toilet seats, and using the same drinking glass or towels.

Hershey highway   noun phrase. slang.   The rectum, when used for anal intercourse. *Hershey* comes from the name of a famous chocolate candy bar.

Hershey squirts   noun phrase, plural.   Diarrhea. Frequent and watery bowel movements.

heterosexual   (hĕt´ ur ō sĕk´ shū ŭl)   noun, adjective. formal, general use.   Someone who prefers sexual relations with a member of the opposite sex. The opposite of homosexual (attracted to the same sex as oneself).

* **hi . . .**   Greeting.   When drawled slowly, with a gentle smile, homosexuals can identify each other by the tone of voice without needing to say anything else.

hickey   (hĭ´ kē)   noun. slang.   A purple or reddish mark that results from passionate sucking on the skin, usually in the neck, shoulder, and chest area.

---

* high beams on (hī bēmz ŏn) noun phrase. slang. When a woman's nipples are erect and noticeable through her clothing. "Take a look at that one. She's got her *high beams on.*"

hind end noun. slang. The buttocks.

* hold it verb phrase. general use. To control one's need to have a bowel movement or to urinate. "I can't *hold it* till we get home. Could you stop at a gas station so I can use the rest room?"

* hole noun. vulgar. The vagina.

homosexual (hō mō sĕk´shū ŭl) noun, adjective. formal, general use. 1. A male who is attracted to, and prefers to have sexual relations with, other males. 2. Any person, male or female, who prefers sexual relations with persons of the same sex.

homo (hō mō) noun. slang (derogatory). A homosexual.

* hooker (hŏŏ kur) noun. slang. A prostitute. "You can walk down Eighth Avenue near 42nd Street and see all the *hookers* waiting for customers."

* horn noun. slang. Penis.

* horny (hor´nē) adjective. slang. Desiring sexual activity. "Z. is the *horniest* man she ever dated. He made love to her twenty times in the past week." "M. was feeling *horny.*"

* hot adjective. slang. Aroused sexually. "She was *hot* and breathing hard." "'I'm so *hot* for you,' he whispered."

hot flashes (hŏt flăsh´ĭz) noun, plural. general use. A symptom that sometimes accompanies the menopause in middle-aged women. The whole body may suddenly feel a quick flash of heat. "B. complained to her doctor about the *hot flashes* she was having."

hot number noun. slang. A cute and sexy woman.

hot shit noun. vulgar. Important person. Used in a derogatory sense. "F. thinks he's *hot shit*, but in my opinion, he's a big zero."

hot to trot (hŏt tū trŏt) adjective. slang. Ready for sexual activity.

hump (hŭmp) verb. vulgar. Have sexual intercourse with.

---

* **hung, to be hung like a mule**   vulgar.   To have a penis and testicles the size of a mule's. (A mule is a large animal like a horse.) "D. is *hung* like a horse." "V. is really *hung*." (He has very large genitals.)

* **hustler** (hŭs´ lur)   noun. slang.   A prostitute.

hymen (hī´ mŭn)   noun. formal.   The membrane (skin) that partly covers the vagina before a woman's first sexual intercourse.   An unbroken *hymen* is considered to be a sign of virginity.   This is no longer as important in American society as it was two generations ago.

hysterectomy (hĭs´ tur ek´ tŭ mē)   noun. formal.   A surgical operation to remove the uterus.

i

illegitimate (ĭl´ lŭ jĭ´ tĭ mĭt)   adjective. formal.   Not legal; not within marriage.   "C. had three *illegitimate* children before she married S."

* **impotent** (ĭm´ pŭ tĭnt)   adjective. formal, general use.   Unable to get or keep an erection long enough to have successful sexual intercourse.

impotence (ĭm´ pŭ tĭns)   noun. formal.   The inability to have sexual intercourse. "G. went to a doctor to get help for his *impotence.*"

impregnate (ĭm prĕg´ nāt)   verb. formal.   To make a female pregnant.   "A single man is capable of *impregnating* thousands of women."

incest (ĭn´ sĕst)   noun. formal, general use.   Sexual relations with a blood relative: parent and child, brother and sister, etc.   The law forbids marriage between close relatives. Incest is a sexual relationship between people who are so closely related that they would not be allowed to marry.

incontinent (ĭn kŏn´ tĭ nĕnt)   adjective. formal, medical use.   Unable to control the flow of urine from the bladder.   "The elderly woman was embarrassed because she was *incontinent* and often urinated when she laughed or sneezed."   This term may also refer to inability to control defecation.

infertility (ĭn´ fur tĭl ĭ tē) noun. formal. Inability to have children. "After four years of marriage with no children, D. and his wife went to an *infertility* clinic to get medical help."

infidelity (ĭn´ fĭ dĕl ĭ tē) noun. general use. Unfaithfulness. Sex with a partner who is not one's own husband or wife. "H. accused his wife of *infidelity* when he found out she had been seeing an old boyfriend."

* **innocent** (ĭn´ ŭ sĕnt) adjective. euphemism. Inexperienced sexually. "H. was *innocent* until she was nineteen years old."

* **intercourse** (ĭn´ tur kors) noun. formal, general use. 1. Human or business relations or communications. 2. *Sexual intercourse.* "Some newly married couples have *intercourse* twice or more a day."

* **intimate** (ĭn´ tĭ mĭt) adjective. 1. general use. Emotionally or physically close. "L. is my *intimate* friend." 2. euphemism. Sexually intimate. "B. and R. were *intimate* before they were married."

* **irregular** (ĭ rĕg´ yū lur) adjective. euphemism. 1. Con-stipated; have difficulties in defecation. Not having regular bowel movements. "O. takes hot water and lemon juice in the morning whenever she is *irregular*." 2. Having irregular menstrual periods.

* **it** noun. slang, euphemism. 1. Sex appeal. "L. has *"it."* 2. The male sex organ. The penis. 3. The female sex organs. The vagina. 4. *do it, make it, make it with;* = have sexual intercourse.

* **itch, the seven-year itch** noun. slang. The desire for sexual experience with a woman other than one's wife. A married man is said to be satisfied with his own wife for the first seven years of marriage, and then he begins to look around at other women, and "itch" to have relations with them. "J. has the *seven-year itch* and he's only been married two years!"

I.U.D. (ĭ yū dē) noun. formal, medical use. An *intrauterine device* (ĭn´ trŭ yū´ tur ĕn dē vīs). A method of birth control. The device is a specially shapped plastic and metal loop which is permanently inserted into a woman's uterus by a doctor. It prevents pregnancy.

j

jack off   (jăk awf)   verb. vulgar.   Masturbate.

jail bait   (jāl´ bāt´)   noun. slang.   A girl under the legal "age of consent" (which is different in each state). If a man over the legal age has sexual intercourse with a girl under the age, he may be accused of rape. This may happen even if the girl was a willing partner. This is called statutory rape (sta chu tor e rap). The punishment is up to 20 years in jail.

jerk off   (jerk awf)   verb. vulgar.   Masturbate.

Jesus   (jē´ zĭ z)   noun. restricted.   In Christian religion, Jesus is the name of the son of God. The name Jesus may be used in any informative discussion of Jesus or his teachings, but it is forbidden to use the name Jesus in a disrespectful manner.

Jesus Christ   (krīst)   noun. restricted use.   The one appointed by God to be the Savior. The Christian church forbids the use of the name in disrespectful ways.   *Jesus, Jesus Christ, Christ* are often used in expressions of surprise, anger, and pain (in spite of the church's restrictions).

Jesus-freak   (jē´ zĭ z frēk)   noun. slang (offensive).   A person who has joined a sect of Christianity that requires him or her to leave their family, collect money from the public, and try to convert others.

jism   (jĭ zm)   noun. slang.   Semen.

jock itch   (jŏk ĭch)   noun. slang.   An itchy rash in the crotch area between the legs. It is caused by heavy sweating.

jockstrap   (jŏk străp)   noun. slang.   An athletic supporter. A garment used to support the male genitals and protect them from injury during athletic activities, games, sports, etc.

* **john**   noun. slang. 1. The bathroom. 2. A prostitute's customer

* **joint**   (joint)   noun. vulgar.   The penis.

* **joystick**   (joi´ stĭk)   noun. vulgar.   The penis.

* **jugs**   (jŭgz)   noun, plural. slang.   A woman's breasts.

k

ka ka (kŏ kŏ) noun. children's language. Feces.

make ka ka verb phrase. Defecate.

keester (kēs´ tur) noun. slang. The buttocks.

* **kinky** (kĭn kē) adjective. slang. 1. Unusual, experimental, strange, as in *kinky* sex. "George always dressed like a woman to make love to his wife. That seemed *kinky* to her. She enjoyed being tied to the bed, which seemed *kinky* to George." 2. Homosexual.

* **knob** (nŏb) noun. slang. Penis

* **knockers** noun. plural. 1. A woman's breasts. 2. Testicles.

knock up verb. vulgar. To get a woman pregnant. "J. *knocked up* his girlfriend and was afraid his wife would find out."

to get knocked up To become pregnant. "C.'s daughter *got knocked up* so C. forced T. to marry her."

* **know** verb. archaic use. Have sexual intercourse with. This is the term used in the Christian Bible. "...And Adam *knew* his wife and she brought forth Cain." It is now used as a euphemism, jokingly. A: "I *knew* Sally as a child." B: "In the Biblical sense?" A: "No, just as friends."

l

labia (lā´ bē ŭ) noun. formal, medical use. The folds of flesh around the vagina.

lady of easy virtue (ē´ zē vur´ chū) noun. euphemism. A prostitute.

lady of the night noun. euphemism. A prostitute.

latrine (lŭ trēn´) noun. army use. Toilet.

lavatory (lă´ vŭ tor´ ē) noun. euphemism. Toilet. (This word comes from the French and means "washroom." Do not confuse with *laboratory*, a place where scientists work.)

* **lay** (lā) 1. verb. vulgar. Have sexual intercourse. "He *laid* her twice." "She wanted to *get laid*." 2. noun. vulgar. The quality of a woman as a sexual partner. "C. looked like a good *lay* to him." "'To be a good *lay*, a woman should have a nice body and have a passionate nature,' he said."

laxative (lăks´ ŭ tǐv) noun. general use. A food or medicine that causes or promotes a bowel movement. "Dried fruit such as prunes act as a *laxative* for most people." "K. was constipated, so she used a *laxative* that her doctor recommended."

lead in one's pencil, to have (lĕd) vulgar. To have the ability to get and keep a firm erection. "Hey T., have some fish. It *puts lead in your pencil*."

lecher (lĕch´ ur) noun. general use. A person who has strong sexual desires for women. This word has a derogatory meaning implying that there is something immoral in the person's needs, or that he is vulgar in his attentions to women.

lechery noun. general use. Excessive (too much) sexual interest or activity. "A very proper and strictly religious person might think that there is too much *lechery* in the world today."

lecherous (lĕch´ ur ŭs) adjective. general use. Having strong sexual desires. This word is used by someone who is *not* interested in the attention of such a person. "J. is a *lecherous* old fool,' said M."

lesbian (lĕz´ bē ĭn) noun. formal, general use. A female homosexual.

lewd (lūd) adjective. general use (derogatory). Lustful. Interested in sex.

library noun. slang. The bathroom. (Because many people read in the bathroom, and keep books and magazines there.)

* **lie with** verb phrase. euphemism. Have sexual intercourse with.

in the life noun phrase. euphemism. Living in the culture of homosexuals and lesbians.

live in sin verb phrase. euphemism for fornicate (derogatory). To live as man and wife without being married to each other. According to religious teachings, this is a *sin*, or crime against God's laws. "Mrs. J. refused to visit her daughter because she felt that she was *living in sin* with her boyfriend."

---

* **live together** verb phrase. euphemism. Live as husband and wife in the same home without being married to each other. No derogatory judgement is implied in this word. "R. and T. *lived together* for three years before they got married."

* **loins** (loinz) noun, plural. euphemism. The reproductive parts. The crotch area.

* **loose** (lūs) adjective. euphemism. Promiscuous. Having many sex partners or not careful in the choice of sexual partners.

* **lungs** noun, plural. slang. A woman's breasts. (Among men) "Did you see the pair of *lungs* on that singer?"

* **lust** (lŭst) 1. verb. general use. To have sexual desire. "X. *lusts* after all big-breasted women." 2. noun. general use. Strong sexual desire. "Sexy movies are made to arouse *lust*."

m

* **madam** (mă´ dŭm) noun. general use. A woman who manages a house of prostitution.

maidenhead (mā´ dĭn hĕd) noun. euphemism. The hymen, a flap of skin that partly covers the vagina before a woman has her first sexual intercourse.

* **make** verb. slang. Have sexual intercourse with. "J. has *made* 75% of all the girls he's dated." "I can be *made*."

make it with verb phrase. slang. Have a successful relationship, including sexual relations. "B. would like to *make it with* S. but she doesn't seem to care for him."

make love (to) verb phrase. euphemism. Have sexual intercourse (with). This expression implies tenderness and affectionate emotion besides the simply physical act. "S. and T. had a beautiful evening: first they ate at a fine restaurant, they saw a good movie, and finally then went home and *made love*."

make out (with) verb phrase. slang. Spend time hugging, kissing, and petting (touching). "Lots of teenagers go to drive in movies just to *make out*."

make out artist   noun. slang.   A person who enjoys making out, possibly with a different girl on each occasion. "Is this your first date with G? Be careful, he's known as a real *make out artist*."

mammary glands   (măm´ ur ē glănz)   noun, plural. formal, medical use.   The breasts. The glands that produce milk for newborn babies. "All mammals have *mammary glands* to produce milk for their young."

man in the boat   noun phrase. slang.   Clitoris.

maricon   (mar ē kŏn)   noun. vulgar, from the Spanish (derogatory).   Homosexual.

masochism   (mă´ sō kǐz m)   noun. formal, general use. A perversion in which a person (a masochist) receives pleasure from pain, insult, or being badly treated. "A *masochist* may want his sex partner to tie him with ropes and beat him with a leather strap."

* **massage parlour**   (mŭ sŏzh´ par´ lur)   noun. euphemism. House of prostitution.

masturbate   (măs´ tur bāt)   verb. formal, general use. To touch and stimulate one's own genitals in order to have an orgasm.

  masturbation   (măs´ tur bā shŭn)   noun form.

* **mate**   (māt)   noun. general use.   1. A sexual partner, a husband or wife. A more or less permanent lover and companion. A man may refer to his wife as his "mate"; this implies an affectionate feeling toward her. "Thanks for the dinner invitation; I'll let you know if we can come as soon as I talk with my *mate*." 2. An animal's sexual partner in producing young ones. "It's mating season; all the male deer are looking for *mates*." 3. verb. general use.   To copulate for the purposes of producing babies or young ones, as animals do. "J.'s pure-bred Siamese cat ran out of the house and *mated* with an ugly old alley cat."

* **meat**   noun. vulgar.   The penis.

  beat the meat   (bēt thŭ mēt)   verb phrase. vulgar. Masturbate.

meat house   noun. vulgar.   House of prostitution.

* **member**   noun. euphemism.   The penis.

ménàge à trois (mā nŏzh´ ŏ trwŏ) noun. slang. Three partners having sexual intercourse. "S. invited his girlfriend and her sister on a date. It was his fantasy to have a *"ménàge à trois."*

menarchy (mĕn´ ar kē) noun. formal, medical use. The time when a girl begins to menstruate. "The average age of *menarchy* among American girls is 12.4 years."

menopause (mĕn´ ō pawz) noun. formal, general use. The end of a woman's child-bearing years, when menstruation stops and ovaries stop producing female sex hormones. "Most women go through *menopause* between 42 and 55 years of age."

mess verb. euphemism. To have a bowel movement in a diaper, in one's underwear, or in any other inappropriate place. "The baby *messed* (in) his diaper." "The child *messed* her pants." "The dog *messed* in the living room."

micturate (mĭk´ tur āt) verb. formal, medical use. Urinate.

middle leg noun. slang. The penis.

* **milkers** noun, plural. vulgar. A woman's breasts.

* **the Milky Way** noun. slang. A woman's breasts.

missionary position (mĭsh´ ĭn ār´ ē pŭ zi´ shŭn) noun. slang. The position for sexual intercourse where the man lies on top of the woman. Some natives in Africa who generally practice rear-entry intercourse were surprised at the manner in which the white missionaries performed sexual intercourse and labeled it the *missionary position*. (A missionary is a person sent by a Christian church to teach about Christianity.)

miss a period verb phrase. general use. To not have a menstrual period on schedule. "Doctor, I *missed my period*. I think I might be pregnant."

* **mistress** (mĭs´ trĭs) noun. general use. A woman who has a permanent relationship with a man, but is not married to him, is his *mistress*. "'I'd rather be a man's *mistress* than his wife,' said G."

molest (mō lĕst´) verb. general use. To bother, annoy, or harm a woman or child in a sexual manner. "Many women do not walk outside alone at night. They are afraid of being *molested*." "Officer! Arrest that man! He *molested* me!"

Montezuma's revenge (mǒn´ tǔ zū´ mǔz rē věnj´) noun. slang. Diarrhea that one gets from visiting Mexico, where it is not safe for foreigners to drink the water.

* **monthly** noun. euphemism. Menstrual period. "B. doesn't like to play tennis when she has her *monthly*."

* **mood, to be in the** euphemism. To be ready for sexual activity. "Not tonight, Honey, I'm *not in the mood*."

* **moon** noun. slang. The buttocks. Teenage and college use.

  hang a moon (hăng ǔ mūn) verb phrase. vulgar. To pull down one's underpants and bend over, showing one's buttocks, out of a window.

  mother-fucker noun. vulgar. 1. A detestable, hateful person. This word is among the most vulgar of American expressions to those who hear it for the first time. However, the original meaning — a person who fucks his mother — is hardly ever thought of. "'Old Man R. is the rottenest, meanest *mother-fucker* who ever walked on earth,' said C." 2. An old friend; a buddy. "I was in big trouble until K. came along. That *mother-fucker* saved my life."

* **mother** noun. vulgar. Short for mother-fucker.

  move one's bowels (mūv wǔnz boulz) verb phrase. general use. Defecate. "I haven't *moved my bowels* for three days; I wonder if I should take a laxative."

* **muff** noun. vulgar. Woman's pubic area.

* **muff-diving** vulgar. Cunnilingus. Oral sex on a woman.

n

* **neck** verb. slang. Spend time hugging and kissing. "They went to a drive-in movie and *necked* through the whole show."

  necrophiliac (něk´ rō fē´ lē ăk) noun. formal. A pervert who has sexual intercourse with a dead body.

neuter (nū´ tur) 1. adjective. general use. Neither male nor female. Not having sexual characteristics. 2. verb. euphemism. To castrate or spay an animal. To remove the sex glands so the animal cannot reproduce.

nipples (nǐp´ ŭlz) noun, plural. general use. 1. The little bumps in the center of the breasts. 2. The rubber mouthpiece on a baby's bottle.

nocturnal emission (nŏk tur´ nŭl ē mǐsh´ ŭn) noun. formal. Ejaculation of semen during sleep. It often accompanies a dream about sexual contact. "Y. dreamed he was holding a beautiful woman in his arms, making love to her. He awoke to find himself wet with semen; he had a *nocturnal emission.*"

nookie (nŏŏ´ kē) noun. vulgar. 1. Sexual intercourse. 2. The vagina. "R. went out looking for *nookie.*" "'How about a little *nookie* tonight?' F. asked her."

* **number one** noun. children's euphemism. Urine. "Daddy, I have to *make number one.*

* **number two** noun. children's euphemism. Feces. *make number two, do number two* verb phrases. Defecate. "The baby did *number two* in his pants."

* **nuts** (nŭts) noun, plural. 1. vulgar. Testicles. 2. slang. Expression of disgust or disappointment. "Oh *nuts*, the movie I wanted to see isn't playing anymore."

nymphomaniac (nǐm´ fō mā´ nē ăk) noun. formal, general use. A woman with unusually strong desires for sexual intercourse. She may have many sex partners, and still not be satisfied. She is suffering from *nymphomania.* 2. slang. A strongly sexed woman.

O

obscene (ŏb sēn´) adjective. general use. Disgusting, offensive. Not acceptable to the moral standards of the community. Pictures of naked bodies may be considered *obscene* by one group of people and beautiful by another group of people.

obscene language = Vulgar language. Some people may think this book is *obscene*, and others will think it is educational.

obscenity (ŏb sĕn´ ĭ tē) noun. An obscene or disgusting thing. A vulgar word. "H. walked away from the argument muttering *obscenities*."

obstetrician (ŏb´ stĕ trĭ´ shŭn) noun. formal, general use. A doctor who specializes in caring for pregnant women and delivering babies.

off-color adjective. slang. Having sexual meanings that are possibly offensive to some people. "G. told an *off-color* joke at the meeting. Instead of laughter, there was a cold silence."

* **old maid** noun. slang (derogatory). An older unmarried woman. This term is becoming obsolete. Many women are choosing not to get married. They prefer to be called "career women."

* **one-eyed worm** (wŭn īd wurm) noun. slang. The penis.

one-night-stand noun. slang. A sexual relationship that lasts for only one evening. There are no emotional feelings between the partners. (This expression comes from show-business slang: A traveling show may spend only one night in a small town; this is called a *one-night-stand*.) "L. was tired of *one-night-stands*; he wanted to meet a woman he could love and have a permanent relationship with."

opposite sex, the (ŏ´ pŭ zĭt sĕx) noun. general use. The other sex. For a man, a woman is the *opposite sex*. "Teenagers begin to take great interest in the *opposite sex*."

oral-genital (or´ ŭl jĕn´ ĭ tŭl) adjective. formal. Mouth to penis or mouth to clitoris sexual stimulation. "Many couples enjoy *oral-genital* sex."

oral sex See "oral-genital."

* **organ** (or´ gŭn) noun. euphemism. Sex organ. The penis.

orgasm (or´ găzm) noun. formal, general use. Sexual climax in male or female. The moment of ejaculation for a male; the rhythmic involuntary vaginal contractions in a female. "S. found it difficult to reach *orgasm*."

* **orgy** (or´ jē) noun. common use. 1. Excess (more than enough) activity in eating, sex, or other pleasures. 2. A party at which a great deal of uninhibited sexual activity occurs. Often used in a joking, exaggerated way.

outhouse noun. slang. A small building that houses an outdoor toilet.

out of wedlock phrase. formal. Referring to children born to an unmarried mother. "She had a child out of *wedlock*, but later married the father."

ova (ō´ vŭ) noun. plural (singular form: ovum). formal medical, general use. The female reproductive cell (egg). "A single *ovum* is released by the ovary each month."

ovary (ō´ vur ē) noun. formal, general use. The female organ that produces the ova. A woman has two *ovaries*, located in the abdomen.

* **oven** (ŭ vĭn) noun. slang. Womb, uterus. "He's got one kid already, and one *in the oven* (that is, his wife is pregnant)."

* **overcoat** noun. slang. Condom.

ovulation (ŏ´ vyū lā´ shŭn) noun. formal, medical use. The monthly release of an ovum from the ovary. "*Ovulation* does not occur before a young girl reaches puberty (sexual maturing)."

p

* **package** (păk´ ĭj) noun. slang. A man's genitals. "His bathing suit is tight, so you can tell he has a nice *package*."

* **pair** noun. slang. A woman's breasts. "The barmaid has quite a *pair*, hasn't she?"

* **pansy** (păn´ zē) noun. slang (derogatory). A male homosexual with effeminate dress and mannerisms. "D. put on a flowered shirt. 'You look like a *pansy*,' his friend said." (A pansy is a small, multicolored flower.)

panther piss noun. vulgar. Cheap, poor quality whisky or beer.

panties (păn´ tēz) noun, plural. general use. Women's or girls' underpants.

Pap smear (păp smēr) noun. formal, medical use. A test for cancer of the cervix. During a woman's pelvic examination at a gynecologist's office, a small sample of the cells of the cervix is obtained, to be tested in the laboratory. "Women are advised to have a *Pap smear* once a year."

pass gas verb phrase. general use. Expel gas from the rectum.

passion (pă´ shŭn) noun. general use. Great emotion. Strong desire for sex.

passionate (pă´ shŭn ŭt) adjective. general use. Very emotional. Having intense feelings. (These may be anger, love, or sexual excitement.)

pecker (pĕk´ ur) noun. vulgar. The penis.

pecker tracks (traks) noun. vulgar. Stains on the front of a man's underwear from dried semen.

peddle one's ass verb phrase. vulgar. To sell sexual favors for money. Work as a prostitute.

pederast (pĕd´ ur ăst) noun. formal. A homosexual man who has relations with a young boy.

pederasty (pĕd´ ur ăs tē) noun. formal. Sexual relations between a man and a young boy. "The police arrested the man and charged him with *pederasty*."

pedophilia (pĕd ō fēl´ ya) noun. formal. Loving children in a sexual way. A *pedophiliac* is a person suffering from *pedophilia*.

pee verb. vulgar. Urinate. "The dog *pee'd* all over the floor." 2. noun. vulgar. Urine.

pee pee (pē pē) 1. verb. children's word. Urinate. "Mommy, I have to *pee pee* real bad." 2. noun. children's word. Urine. "There's *pee pee* on the floor." 3. noun. children's word. Penis.

peeping Tom (pē pĭng tŏm) noun. slang. A pervert who gets pleasure from secretly looking (peeping) in windows to watch women get undressed, or watch couples engage in sexual activities. A voyeur.

pelvic examination (pĕl´ vĭk ĕg zăm´ ĭn ā shŭn) noun. formal, general use. An examination, through the vagina, of a woman's internal reproductive organs. "D. went to the doctor for a *pelvic examination* to see if her uterus had returned to normal after her pregnancy."

pendejo (pĕn dā´ hō) noun. vulgar (Spanish). 1. Pubic hair. 2. A very stupid, clumsy person.

* **penetration** (pĕn ŭ trā´ shŭn) noun. formal. The act of entering; the entering of the vagina by the penis. "*Penetration* is difficult or impossible without a firm erection of the penis."

* **period** (pēr´ ē ŭd) noun. general use. The menstrual period. The time of the month when a woman's uterus releases the lining and blood that has been building up in it. "H.'s *period* usually lasted six last days." "Her *period* was late."

miss a period Not have a monthly period. "Doctor, I've *missed two periods*. Do you think I might be pregnant?"

perversion (pur vur´ zhŭn) noun. general use. A sexual practice that is considered unusual and possibly unpleasant to a majority of people. Many common sexual acts were considered *perversions* by our grandparents.

* **pervert** (pur´ vurt) noun. general use (derogatory). A person who engages in some form of perversion or unnatural sexual activity.

* **pet** verb. slang. To arouse to passion by gentle fondling (touching) of skin, breasts, and genitals.

* **peter** (pē´ tur) noun. children's language. The penis.

piddle (pĭd´ ŭl) verb. euphemism. Urinate. "The puppy *piddled* whenever it was excited."

piece of ass noun. vulgar. 1. A woman, seen as a sexual object only. "'L. is a nice *piece of ass*,' said R." 2. An act of sexual intercourse without emotional involvement. "'If I don't get a *piece of ass* soon, I'll explode!' he said."

piece of tail Same as piece of ass.

piece Short for *piece of ass* or *piece of tail*. "How about a little *piece* tonight?"

piece of shit   noun. vulgar.   Any worthless, useless thing. "That new motorcycle I bought is a *piece of shit;* it has been in the repair shop six times since I got it."   "D. felt like a *piece of shit* when he arrived at the party.   He was the only person who had not brought a gift."

* **piles**   (pīlz)   noun. general use.   Hemorrhoids.   Swollen or varicose veins in the region of the anus.

* **pill, the**   noun. general use.   A daily pill containing female hormones taken for the purpose of preventing pregnancy.   A birth control method.   The hormone causes ovulation to stop. "O. was *on the pill,* so she wasn't afraid of getting pregnant."

pimp   (pĭmp)   noun. slang.   The man who manages one or more prostitutes.   He finds customers for her and bails her out of jail when she is arrested.   She in turn pays him all or a percentage of her fees.

pinch a loaf   verb phrase. vulgar.   Defecate.

* **pipe**   noun. slang.   Penis.

pish   (pĭsh)   verb. children's word.   Urinate.

piss   1. verb. vulgar.   Urinate.   2. noun. vulgar.   Urine.

piss away   verb phrase. vulgar.   To waste.   To spend money without thinking.   "L. inherited a fortune from his rich uncle but he *pissed it away* on foolish things."

pissed off   adjective. vulgar.   Angry.   "S. got *pissed off* when he heard that W. had taken his car without asking for permission."   *That pisses me off.*   That makes me angry.

p.o.'d   (pē ōd)   slang.   Abbreviation for pissed off.   "'No need to get *p.o.'d,*' he said, 'I'll fix what I broke.'"

pisser   noun. slang.   1. A remarkable, daring, or amusing person or child.   "Young W.D. is a real *pisser.*   He's only four years old but he already loves to flirt with girls."   2. A difficult job.   "Fixing the refrigerator was a real *pisser.*   We didn't have any of the right tools."

piss on that   exclamation. vulgar.   An expression of disagreement or disapproval of a suggestion made by another.

platonic   (plŭ tŏn´ ĭk)   adjective. general use.   This refers to a friendship between male and female that does not include sex.   "She had a *platonic* relationship with him for years."

---

play "hide the sausage" verb phrase. slang. Have sexual intercourse. (Male to male friend) "My wife and I are going home after the movie to play *'hide the sausage.'*"

play with oneself verb phrase. slang. Masturbate. Contrast with *play by himself*: To play alone, without friends. Be careful. *The child played by himself* has no dangerous meanings. *The child played with himself* means he was masturbating.

* **play pocket pool** verb phrase. slang. To masturbate or stimulate oneself through the pants pocket.

play the skin flute verb phrase. slang. Oral sex. Fellatio. Suck a man's penis. Also, *play the pink piccolo.*

* **poop, poo poo** (pūp, pū pū) children's language. 1. noun. Feces. 2. verb. Defecate.

poop chute (pūp shūt) noun. vulgar, humorous. The anus.

pornography (porn ŏ´ grŭ fē) noun. formal, general use. Stories, movies, books, and pictures that tell or show scenes of sexual activities. The purpose of *pornography* is to sexually arouse a person. "Q. was arrested for selling *pornography* to children."

pornographic (por nŏ´ grăf ĭk) adjective form. "N. enjoyed *pornographic* movies."

* **possess** (pō zĕs´) verb. euphemism. Have sexual intercourse with a woman. Found in women's romance novels, and in books printed before stronger language was allowed.

posterior (pŏs tēr´ ē ur) noun. euphemism. The buttocks.

* **potency** (pō´ tŭn sē) noun. formal, general use. A man's ability to perform sexual intercourse. "X.'s *potency* increased when he started taking vitamins."

potty (pŏ´ tē) noun. children's word. Toilet. A small toilet especially for training little children. It has a removable pot.

powder room (pou´ dur rŭm) noun. euphemism. The bathroom. This word is used by women, generally in restaurants or other public places. They may excuse themselves to go "powder my nose" (apply facial makeup or cosmetics).

pregnancy (prĕg´ nŭn sē) noun. formal, general use. The nine-month period during which a baby grows in its mother's uterus.

premature ejaculation (prē´ mŭ chur´ ē jă k´ yū lā shŭn) noun. formal. This is when a man reaches climax (ejaculation) before or quickly after the penis enters the vagina.

* **prick** (prĭk) noun. vulgar. 1. The penis. 2. A disliked person (male).

privates, private parts (prī´ vĭ ts, prī´ vĭ t parts) noun, plural. euphemism. The genital area of a man or woman.

proctologist (prŏk tŏl´ ŭ jĭst) noun. formal. A doctor who specializes in treating diseases of the rectum and anus.

procurer (prō kyū´ rur) noun. formal. A person who persuades women to work as prostitutes. One who finds a suitable prostitute for a particular customer.

profanity (prō făn´ ĭ tē) noun. general use. Vulgar words and expressions. Words and expressions that are forbidden by Christian church teachings. "Don't use *profanity* in the classroom."

promiscuous (prō mĭs´ kyū ŭs) adjective. general use. This word describes a person who has sexual intercourse with many different partners, and who may not be very careful in choosing a partner. "A *promiscuous* person may easily get a venereal disease."

prophylactic (prō fĭl ăk´ tĭk) noun. general use. A condom. A birth control device worn by the man on the penis.

* **proposition** (prŏ´ pŭ zĭ´ shĭn) 1. verb. euphemism. To suggest sexual activity with a person. "May was so attractive that men would walk up to her on the street or in the subway and *proposition* her." "B. was at her new job just three days when her boss *propositioned* her." 2. noun. euphemism. The suggestion of sexual activity. "A man made a *proposition* to her at the party, but she told him to get lost."

prostate (prŏ´ stāt) noun. formal, general use. The gland in a man that surrounds the urethra near the bladder.

puberty (pū´ bur tē) noun. formal, general use. The period of time when children develop adult sexual abilities and characteristics. This includes the period of breast growth and the beginning of menstruation in girls; the growth of the sex organs, beginnings of ejaculations, deepening voice, etc. in boys. "The average girl reaches *puberty* at age eleven."

pubic area (pyū´ bĭk ār´ ē ŭ) noun. formal, general use. The crotch. The lower part of the abdomen.

pubic hair (pyū´ bĭk hār) noun. formal, general use. The hair in the pubic area.

pudendum (pū dĕn´ dŭm) noun. formal, medical use. The vulva. The female genital area.

* **pussy** (poō´ sē) noun. vulgar. The vagina.

* **put out (for)** verb. vulgar. Give sexual favors (said of a woman). to allow someone to have sexual intercourse. "N. is a married woman, but she *puts out for* all her old boyfriends."

q

* **queen** noun. slang. A male homosexual with feminine appearance and manners.

queer (kwēr) 1. noun. slang (derogatory). A homosexual. 2. adjective. Homosexual.

quickie (kwĭk´ ē) noun. slang. A fast session of sexual intercourse. "Do we have time for a *quickie* before going to the movies?"

r

* **rag** noun. slang. Sanitary napkin.

to be on the rag To be having one's period. To be irritable and bitchy. This may be said even of men.

rape (rāp) verb. general use. To force sexual intercourse with a woman. *Rape* is a crime.

rape artist (rāp´ ar´ tĭst) noun. slang. A man who rapes women. A rapist.

rapist (rāp´ ĭst) noun. formal, general use. A man who forces sexual intercourse with a woman. "The police are looking for the *rapist* who raped and killed five women."

reach a climax (rēch´ ŭ klĭ măks) verb phrase. general use. Have an orgasm.

* **rear, rear end** noun. euphemism. The buttocks.

rectum (rĕk´ tŭm) noun. formal, general use. The last part of the large colon, or large intestine. "The feces are kept in the *rectum* until defecation."

red-light district noun. euphemism. An area where there are houses of prostitution. "It seems that every town has its *red-light district.*"

* **relations, to have . . . with** verb phrase. euphemism. Have sexual intercourse. "L. divorced his wife because she refused *to have relations* with him."

relieve oneself (rē lēv´ wŭnz sĕlf) verb phrase. euphemism. Urinate. "Is there a public rest room here? If I don't *relieve myself*, I'll explode."

rest room noun. euphemism. A toilet in a public place such as a restaurant, gas station, theater, etc.

rhythm method (rĭ´ thŭm mĕ thŭd) noun. general use. A method of birth control. The partners have sexual intercourse only during the safe, or non-fertile days of the woman's menstrual cycle.

ride the cotton pony verb phrase. vulgar. 1. To wear a sanitary napkin; that is, be menstruating. 2. To have sex with a woman who is menstruating.

* **rocks** noun, plural. vulgar. The testicles.

  get one's rocks off (gĕt wŭnz rŏks awf) verb phrase. vulgar. 1. Ejaculate; reach a sexual climax. 2. Enjoy oneself very much by participating in some hobby or activity. "P. *gets his rocks off* going to the horse races and betting on the horses." "It seems some teachers get their *rocks off* by yelling at students and embarassing them."

Rocky Mountain oysters (rŏ´ kē moun´ tĭn oi´ sturz) noun, plural. Testicles.

* **root** (rūt) noun. slang. A man's penis.

* **rubber** noun. slang. A condom.

---

* **rump** (rŭmp) noun. slang. The buttocks.

rump ranger noun. slang. A homosexual male.

* **run around** verb. euphemism. Have sexual relations with several partners although married to another person. "T. has a beautiful wife. I can't understand why he *runs around.*"

* **runs** noun. slang. Diarrhea. (One has to *run* to the bathroom quickly when one has diarrhea.) "B. ate green apples and they gave him the *runs.*" "Y. stayed home from work because he had the *runs.*"

S

S.B.D. (ĕs bē dē) noun. vulgar. *S*ilent *B*ut *D*eadly. Quiet explosion of gas from the rectum that has a very bad (deadly) smell.

sadist (sā´ dĭst) noun. general use. A person who gets sexual or other pleasure from giving pain to his or her partner.

sadism (sā´ dĭsm) noun. general use. A perversion wherein sexual pleasure is gotten from causing pain to another person.

sadomasochism (sā´ dō mă´ sŭ kĭzm) noun. A sexual perversion in which one partner enjoys causing pain, and the other enjoys being hurt. Also; *S&M.*

* **safe sex** noun. euphemism. Using a condom to prevent spreading the AIDS virus. Avoiding anal intercourse.

* **safety** noun. euphemism. A condom.

sanitary napkin (săn´ ĭ ter´ ē năp´ kĭn) formal, general use. A pad of cotton and gauze used to absorb menstrual blood.

* **satisfy** (săt´ ĭs fī) verb. euphemism. To cause one's partner to reach a sexual climax.

to be satisfied Have a sexual climax.

* **schlong** (shlŏng) noun. vulgar. The penis.

schmuck (schmŭk) noun. 1. slang. A stupid person. 2. vulgar. The penis (Yiddish word). A: "What does she like about M.? He's such a *schmuck!*" B: "Maybe he *has* a big *schmuck?*"

screaming fairy   noun. slang (derogatory).   A homosexual who is very obviously a homosexual. He wears extremely effeminate clothing, and walks and speaks in an exaggeratedly female manner.

* **screw** (skrū)   verb.   1. vulgar. Have sexual intercourse with. "L. is a sex maniac; all he thinks of is *screwing*." 2. slang. Cheat in a business deal. "Don't do business with the company; they'll *screw* you if they can."

screw around   verb phrase. vulgar.   1. Have many sexual partners. "J. is married, but he still *screws around*." 2. Bother or annoy someone. "Please stop *screwing around*. You're interfering with my work."

screw with   Try to cheat in a business or social matter. "Nobody *screws with* Old Mr. Z if they know what's good for them." (If they do not want to have bad things happen to them.)

screw up   verb. slang.   1. Bungle; do an unsatisfactory job; do something incompetently. 2. Cause something to fail. "The secretary *screwed up* again-she was supposed to send a copy of this letter to the customer, but she forgot." "I wanted to go to the beach this weekend, but the bad weather *screwed up* my plans."

screw you! (skrū yū) exclamation. vulgar.   An angry reply to some one.   Similar to *fuck you*, but somewhat less vulgar.

scrotum (skrō´ tŭm)   noun. formal, general use.   The sac that contains the testicles.

* **scum** (skŭm) noun. vulgar. Semen.

scumbag (skŭm´ băg)   noun. vulgar.   1. A condom; a rubber prophylactic used for birth control. 2. A very unlikable person.

* **seat**   noun. euphemism.   The buttocks.

see a man about a horse   verb phrase. slang.   Go to the bathroom.

* **seed** (sēd)   noun. euphemism.   Sperm. Characteristics that can be inherited genetically.

self-abuse (sĕlf´ ŭ by ūs´) noun. euphemism.
Masturbation. This term is left over from more prudish days
when mothers thought that is was harmful for children to
masturbate. They told them that it would make them blind.
In one joke, a boy asks, "Is it alright if I do it only until I need
glasses?"

semen (sē´ mĭn) noun. formal, general use. The white
liquid produced in the male reproductive organs. The fluid
that carries the sperm.

sex (sĕks) noun. general, use. 1. Gender. Maleness or
femaleness. "What *sex* are the new puppies?" "Can the doctor
tell the *sex* of the baby before it is born?" 2. An act of sexual
intercourse. "X. always enjoyed *sex* before breakfast." "L.
would like to have *sex* at least three times a week, but his wife
isn't interested in *sex* that often. 3. The general topic of sexual
matters. "All she talks about is *sex.*"

sex appeal (sĕks´ ŭ pēl) noun. general use.
Attractiveness. "Y. has a lot of *sex appeal;* the girls are always
around him."

sex drive noun. general use. The impulse or need that
causes a person to desire sexual relations. "Some people have
a greater *sex drive* than others." "Does a woman's *sex drive*
increase as she gets older?"

sex fiend (... fēnd) noun. general use. 1. Rapist or
other antisocial pervert. 2. A person with a very strong sex
drive (humorous use).

sex maniac (sĕks mā´ nē ăk) noun. general use. 1.
Rapist, sex fiend. A dangerous person who may murder or
seriously harm his victims. 2. slang. A person with a strong
sex drive (humorous).

sex organs (... or´ gŭnz) noun, plural. general use. 1.
The penis and testicles (male). 2. The vagina and vulva
(female).

sex symbol (... sĭm bŭl) noun. general use. A very
attractive famous male or female. "Marilyn Monroe was the
most famous *sex symbol* in the world in the 1950's."

sexual intercourse (sĕk´ shū ŭl ĭn´ tur kors) noun.
formal, general use. The act of union of the man's body and
the woman's body. "The penis enters the vagina during *sexual
intercourse.*"

sexy (sĕk´ sē) adjective. general use. 1. Attractive, in a sexual way. "He has a *sexy* voice." "That's a *sexy* bathing suit." "W. is a *sexy* woman." 2. Aroused, interested in sex. "H. was feeling *sexy*."

shack up (with) verb. slang. Live in the same home as man and wife without being legally married. (A shack is a cheaply made house.) Somewhat derogatory feelings may be felt by the speaker, but not necessarily. "K. has been *shacking up with* D. for over a year."

* **shaft** (shăft) noun. slang. Penis.

* **shake hands with a friend** verb phrase. vulgar. 1. Urinate. 2. Masturbate.

she-man (shē´ măn´) noun. slang. Homosexual, particularly an effeminate man. Also, *she-male*.

shit (shĭt) noun. vulgar. 1. Feces. 2. Junk, worthless things. 3. Heroin (narcotic drug).

shit verb. vulgar. Defecate.

Shit! Exclamation of anger, disgust or disappointment.

shits, the noun. The runs. Diarrhea. "H. always gets *the shits* when he eats raisins."

shitty (shĭt´ ē) adjective. vulgar. Lousy, no-good, worthless. "How was the movie?" "*Shitty*."

All of these expressions with shit are vulgar:

apeshit (āp´ shĭt) adjective. vulgar. 1. Angry in a crazy, wild, uncontrollable way. "When R. saw his best friend dancing with his girl, he went *apeshit*." 2. Very enthusiastic. Excited and interested in something. "J. goes *apeshit* when he's around racing cars."

beat the shit out of verb phrase. vulgar. 1. To punish by spanking or whipping. "When my father found out I had lied to him, he *beat the shit out of me*." 2. To defeat by a large margin. "The Giants *beat the shit out of* the Green Socks. The score was 12 to 1."

crock of shit noun. vulgar. A lot of lies.

don't give me that shit vulgar expression Don't tell me those lies.

eat this shit   verb phrase. vulgar.   Accept insults and punishments without protesting. "Maybe the boss expects me to *eat this shit*, but I'll quit my job before I take a cut in pay."

full of shit   adjective phrase. vulgar.   Always telling lies or exaggerated stories that are not based on the facts. Empty talk. "Don't listen to Z. He's *full of shit.*"

give a shit   verb phrase. vulgar.   To care, be concerned, have an interest in.   *don't/doesn't give a shit*   To have no interest in or regard for something. "The reason that H. is usually late and doesn't finish his reports is that he just *doesn't give a shit* whether he keeps the job or not."

holy shit   (hō lē shĭt)   vulgar.   Expression of surprise or discovery.

horseshit   noun. vulgar.   Lies, false stories. Same as bullshit.

hot shit   noun. vulgar.   Very important. (Said sarcastically.) "B. thinks she's *hot shit*, but she really has no power in this office."

I'm so happy I could shit   Vulgar expression.   1. I'm very happy. 2. I'm really miserable. (The meaning depends on the context and the tone of voice.)

little shit   noun. vulgar.   A very unimportant person, disliked and usually small in size.

lower than whale shit   adjective phrase. vulgar.   Depressed, sad, humiliated, regretful. "H. lost his job; his girlfriend left him, and his car broke down. 'How do you feel?' asked his friend. '*Lower than whaleshit.*' he said."

no shit!   vulgar.   Exclamation of surprise or disbelief at what someone has just said. It is an expression of appreciation of the unusualness of the news.   A: "My cousin just married a famous movie star."   B: "*No shit!* How did he meet her?" Said sarcastically, "*No shit*" means "You're not telling me anything new. I can see it for myself; everybody already knows that."

piece of shit   noun. vulgar.   A worthless, poorly made thing. "You paid $20 for this clock? It's not worth it; it's a *piece of shit.*"

pile of shit   noun. vulgar.   A lot of lies.

scared shitless   (skard' shĭt' lĭs)   adjective. vulgar.   Very scared.

shit a brick   verb phrase. vulgar.   1. Expel a large mass of feces.   2. Do something very difficult.   "We had to *shit bricks* to build this bridge."   3. Be very surprised, upset, or angry. "When C. learned we had gotten the prize, he was ready to *shit a brick*."

Shit Creek   (shĭt krēk)   noun. vulgar.   A river made of shit.   A very difficult position to be in.   "They were *up Shit Creek without a paddle*."   (They were unable to get out of severe difficulties.

shit-eating grin   noun phrase. vulgar.   A big smile, usually of pride.   "N. walked in the door with this big *shit-eating grin* on his face, and we knew he had gotten the raise he wanted."

shit face   noun. vulgar.   Ugly person.   Used as an insult.

shit-faced   adjective. vulgar.   Drunk.

shit for the birds   noun phrase. vulgar.   Worthless idea or thing.   "I don't think much of that suggestion you made.   It's *shit for the birds*."

shit happens   vulgar expression.   You can expect bad things to happen.   That's life.   Don't get too surprised or upset. (Sign on bumper stickers, tee shirts, etc.)

shit head   (shĭt hěd)   noun. vulgar.   A stupid person.

shit hole   noun. vulgar.   A very undesirable house, home, place.   "We lived in this *shit hole* for three years before we could earn enough to move to a better apartment."

shit list   noun. vulgar.   A list (imaginary) of people whom one is angry with and desires to punish or cause trouble for. "Don't expect favors from Mr. T.   Ever since you insulted his wife, he has had you on his *shit list*."

shitload   (shĭt lōd)   noun. vulgar.   A very great quantity.   I have a *shitload* of work to do tonight."

shit or get off the pot   vulgar.   You are on the only toilet in the house.   If you are not using it, get off so that someone else may use it.   This expression is used in situations where one person is occupying the only position where an action may take place and he is delaying or wasting time, or afraid to take action.   The speaker wants a chance to get into that position so that he might take action.

---

shit on a shingle   noun.   Barbequed beef on a (hamburger) bun.   (A shingle is a flat piece of tar paper used in making the roof of a house.)   2. Army use: creamed chipped beef on toast.

shit out of luck   vulgar.   Good luck has come to an end. Bad luck.   "We tried to find an all-night drug store, but we were *shit out of luck*."   This may be said more politely, "We were S.O.L."

to shit in one's pants   verb phrase. vulgar.   Be very frightened.   "When we saw the bear coming at us, we just about *shit in our pants*."

tough shit   (tŭf shĭt)   vulgar.   Exclamation of a lack of sympathy for someone who has a problem.   Bad luck.   (It's your bad luck, but we do not make any exceptions even in your case.)   "But I must have it today."   "*Tough shit*.   There are ten people ahead of you."   Less strong: *T.S.*

when the shit hits the fan   When the truth becomes known and causes a lot of trouble.   Fan = a machine that blows air to keep people cool.   If shit hits this, the fan will blow shit all over the room and the people in it.   "The newspapers are going to print the story about Congressman X's criminal activities.   I don't want to be around when *the shit hits the fan*."

* **shoot off**   verb. vulgar.   Ejaculate.

shoot one's wad   verb phrase. vulgar.   Ejaculate.

* **short arm**   noun. slang.   The penis.

short arm inspection   verb phrase. slang.   Army usage.   A medical examination to check for venereal disease.

shovel the shit   verb phrase. vulgar.   Tell a great deal of lies.   "D. is good at *shoveling the shit*; he'd be a great salesman."

shove it up your ass   vulgar.   Exclamation of anger toward someone.   "I am not interested in listening to your argument. "You can *shove it up your ass* for all I care."

sinkers and floaters   (sĭn´ kurz ănd flō´ turz)   noun, plural. vulgar.   Feces in the toilet bowl.   Some sink, and some float, hence, *sinkers and floaters*.

sitz bath   (sĭts´ băth)   noun. general use.   Sitting in a tub of warm water with medication in it to treat genital sores, hemorrhoids, or other anal or vulval problems.

sixty-nine   noun.   vulgar euphemism.   Oral-genital relations. Fellatio and cunnilingus at the same time; the bodies appear to be like the numbers 6 and 9.

soixante-neuf   (swă´ sănt   noof)   in French.

skinny dip   (skĭ´ nē   dĭp)   verb.   slang.   Go swimming without a bathing suit.   "They went *skinny dipping* in the moonlight."

slam, bam, thank you ma'am   slang.   Very quick sexual intercourse without pleasure for the female partner.

sleep with   verb.   euphemism.   Have sexual intercourse with.

sleep around   verb.   euphemism.   Have casual sexual relations with several partners.

slut   (slŭt)   noun.   slang (derogatory).   A promiscuous woman; one who has sexual relations with many men and does not use any judgement in choosing her partners.

* **snatch**   (snăch)   noun.   vulgar.   The vagina.

sodomy   (sŏ´ dŭ mē)   noun.   formal and general use. Anal intercourse.   Sex relations with the penis in the anus.

sodomist   A person who performs sodomy.

* **soil**   (soil)   verb.   euphemism.   To dirty with feces.   "The baby has *soiled* its diaper."   "He got so scared when he saw the ghost that he *soiled* his pants."

son of a bitch   noun.   vulgar.   1. Literally, the son of a female dog.   A selfish, hateful person who may deliberately cause unhappiness for others.   "Mr. A. is *a real son of a bitch.* He would sell his own grandmother if he could make a profit from it."   2. A very difficult, time-consuming job.   "Trying to move that heavy piano was a real *son of a bitch.*"   3. An expression to show surprise at an unexpected happening.   "*Son of a bitch!* I never expected to see you in Miami!"   4. Affectionate term for a good friend.   "Hi, you old *son of a bitch*; it's good to see you."   *S.O.B.* is the abbreviation, which is less vulgar.

spay   (spā)   verb.   formal, medical, general use.   To remove a female cat or dog's ovaries so she cannot have babies.   Past tense, spayed   (spād).

sperm   (sperm)   noun.   general use.   The male sex cells. "500,000 sperm are contained in one teaspoon of semen."

spermatazoa   (sper´ mă tŭ zō´ ŭ)   formal.   Sperm.

---

spermicide (spur´ mŭ sīd´) noun. A birth control foam, jelly, or suppository that kills sperm.

* **stacked** (stăkt) adjective. slang. Have large breasts. "L. is really *stacked*. She wears a size 40 E bra."

* **stern** (sturn) noun. slang, euphemism. The buttocks. (The original meaning is the rear part of a boat.)

* **sterile** (stĕr´ ŭl) adjective. formal, general use. Unable to have children. Not fertile.

  sterility (stur´ ĭl ĭ tē´) noun. formal, general use. Inability to have children.

  stinker noun. vulgar. 1. Explusion of intestinal gas. "She let out a real *stinker* at the bar." 2. A disliked person.

* **stool** (stūl) noun. formal, medical use. Feces. "The doctor asked his patient to bring a *stool* sample to the laboratory for testing."

* **stork, the** noun. euphemism. According to traditional stories told to children, the stork (a bird with a very long beak) brings babies. "Mr. and Mrs. Z. are expecting a visit from *the stork*."

* **straight** (strāt) adjective. slang. 1. Not homosexual. Preferring to have sexual relations with the opposite sex. "W. appears effeminate (like a woman) but he's completely *straight*." 2. Having no unusual sexual needs or desires. Not perverted.

  street-walker noun. slang. A prostitute.

  suck (sŭk) verb. vulgar. Perform fellatio.

  Suck my dick! Exclamation of anger similar in intensity to "Shove it up your ass!"

  swallow a watermelon seed verb phrase. slang. Become pregnant. "What happened to your wife? She *swallow a watermelon seed?*"

* **swing** verb. slang. Exchange sexual partners. "Two married couples may get together to *'swing'* for the evening."

  swing both ways verb phrase. slang. To be bisexual. To enjoy sexual relations with one's own sex as well as with the opposite sex.

* **swinger**   noun. slang.   1. A person who knows the up-to-date styles and fads, and who goes to many parties and other social events. 2. A person who does the latest "popular" sexual activities. (This may refer to having more than one partner, being bisexual, taking part in group sex, being willing to experiment with "perversions." etc.) 3. Testicles. 4. A woman's breasts that "swing" when she walks.

* **swish**   verb. slang.   To walk with a very effeminate manner (like a woman). Said of homosexual men. "H. *swished* in with his pink suit and flowered shirt."

  syphilis   (sĭ´ fŭ lĭ s)   noun. formal, medical, general use. A serious disease that is spread through sexual contact. A venereal disease.

t

* **tail**   noun. 1. euphemism.   The buttocks. 2. vulgar.   The vagina.

  piece of tail   (pēs ŭv tāl)   noun. vulgar.   An act of sexual intercourse.

  take a crap   verb phrase. vulgar.   Defecate.

  take a dump   verb phrase. vulgar.   Defecate.

  take a leak   (tāk ŭ lēk)   verb phrase. vulgar.   Urinate.

  take a shit   verb phrase. vulgar.   Defecate.

  tampon   (tăm´ pŏn)   noun. general use.   A tube of cotton that is inserted in the vagina to absorb menstrual blood. "*Tampax*® is a well-known brand of *tampon*."

* **tear off a piece**   verb phrase. vulgar.   Have sexual intercourse.

  teats   (tēts)   noun, plural.   1. general use.   An animal's mammary glands, such as those of a cow or dog. 2. vulgar. A woman's breasts.

  testes   (tĕs´ tēz)   noun, plural.   formal use. *also*

  testicles   (tĕs´ tŭ kulz)   noun, plural. general use.   Both of these terms mean the male reproductive glands located in the scrotum.

---

testosterone (tĕs tŏs´ tur ōn) noun. formal, medical use. A male sex hormone.

that time of the month noun phrase. euphemism. The monthly period. The time of menstruation.

third sex, (the) noun. slang. Homosexual.

* **throne** (thrōn) noun. slang. The toilet. (A throne is the seat of a king.)

* **tinkle** (tĭn´ kŭl) verb. children's word. Urinate.

titties (tĭd´ ēz) noun, plural. children's word: slang. The breasts.

tits (tĭts) noun, plural. slang. The breasts.

toilet (toi´ lĕt) noun. general use. 1. The object one urinates or defecates into, located in the bathroom. 2. The bathroom.

toilet paper noun. general use. A roll of soft tissue paper used in the bathroom.

toilet train verb. general use. To teach a young child to gain control over bowel movements and urination so they may use the toilet. "Mrs. M. began to *toilet train* her son at two and a half, but it was six months before he was completely out of diapers."

toilet water noun. general use. A light cologne (perfume) that is splashed on the body after a bath. (It is *not* water from the toilet, as one might think. This is not a dangerous word.)

tokus (tō´ kĭs) also *tuchus* (tōō´ kĭs) noun. Yiddish euphemism. The buttocks.

* **tonsils** (tŏn´ sĭlz) noun, plural. vulgar. A woman's breasts.

* **tool** (tūl) noun. vulgar. The penis.

topless (top´ lĭs) adjective. general use. Naked (with no clothes on) above the waist (said of a woman). "J. went to a *topless* bar." (That is, where the waitresses were topless.) "*Topless* bathing suits are not allowed on public beaches in New Jersey."

tough titty (tŭf tĭ´ dē) vulgar expression. That's too bad, but it's all you deserve. Life is like that for all of us.

transvestite (trănz věs´tĭt) noun. formal, general use. A person who prefers to dress in the clothes of the opposite sex. Both heterosexuals and homosexuals may be transvestites. This is socially acceptable for women, but not for men.

* **trick** noun. slang (used by prostitutes). A paid act of sexual intercourse. "She *turned seven tricks* that night."

tubal ligation (tū´bŭl lī´gā´shŭn) noun. formal, medical use. A surgical operation that cuts and ties the fallopian tubes, preventing pregnancy from occuring. Sterilization of the woman.

tush (toosh) also *tushie* noun. euphemism, children's word. The buttocks.

turd (turd) noun. vulgar. A piece of feces.

* **turned on** adjective. slang. Excited, aroused for sexual activity. "'Disco music really *turns me on*,' she said."

twat (twŏt) noun. vulgar. The vagina.

u

undies (ŭn´dēz) noun, plural. euphemism. Underwear.

unmentionables (ŭn měn´shĭn ŭ blz) noun, plural. euphemism. Ladies' underwear.

unwell (ŭn´wĕl) adjective. euphemism. Having one's menstrual period.

ureter (yū rē´tur) noun. formal, medical use. The tube that urine travels from the kidney to the bladder.

urethra (yū rē´thrŭ) noun. formal, medical use. The tube from the bladder to the outside of the body. "Urine is formed in the kidneys, stored in the bladder, and passed out of the body through the *urethra*."

urinate (yoor´ĭ nāt) verb. formal. Expel the waste liquid (urine) from the bladder.

urinal (yoor´ĭ nŭl) noun. general use. An object that men can urinate into while standing in a public men's room.

urine (yoo´rĭn) noun. formal, general use. The waste liquid that is filtered out of the blood.

urogenital (yŏŏ´ rō jěn ĭ tŭl) adjective. formal. Referring to all the genital and urinary organs and functions. *Also*

urinogenital (yŏŏ´ rĭ nō jěn´ ĭ tŭl)

urologist (yŏŏ´ rŏl ŭ jĭst) noun. formal. A doctor who specializes in treating problems involving the kidneys, bladder, penis, and testicles.

used-beer department noun phrase. slang. The bathroom.

uterus (yū´ tur ĭs) noun. formal, general use. The female organ in which a baby may grow. The womb.

V

VD (vē dē) noun. general use. Venereal disease. These are diseases that are spread by sexual contact. "Syphilis and gonorrhea are the two most common *venereal diseases,* but AIDS is the most deadly." "He went to a *VD* clinic to get a blood test for syphilis."

vaginismus (vă´ jĭn ĭz´ mĭs) noun. formal, medical use. A sudden cramping of muscles in the vagina. It happens when a young woman has many fears about sex. This can prevent intercourse. When it happens during sexual intercourse, the man may not be able to get his penis out until the woman is relaxed. Sometimes a doctor is needed to separate the two partners!

vasectomy (vă sěk´ tŭ mē) noun. formal. A surgical procedure to sterilize a man. The urologist (doctor) cuts a piece of the vas deferens. This prevents the sperm from leaving the body through the penis.

venereal disease see VD.

* **vibrator** (vī brā´ tur) noun. general use. An object used to provide sexual pleasure. A battery-powered dildo.

virgin (vur´ jĭn) noun. general use. 1. A woman or man who has not had sexual intercourse. "They were both *virgins* when they got married."

virginity (vur´ jĭn´ ĭ tē) noun. general use. The state of being a virgin. "She lost her *virginity* many years before she got married."

Virgin Mary, the The mother of Jesus Christ. According to Christian teachings, Mary conceived Jesus without having sexual intercourse with any man.

virile (vĭr´ ŭl) adjective. formal, general use. 1. Having the ability to perform sexual intercourse. 2. Manly, strong, brave.

> *virility* (vĭr´ ĭl ĭ tē) noun. formal. The ability to perform sexual intercourse.

* **void** (void) verb. formal. Urinate.

voyeur (voi´ yer) noun. formal. A person who enjoys watching other people get undressed or have sexual intercourse. A "peeping Tom."

vulva (vŭl´ vŭ) noun. formal. The external female sexual parts, including the labia (lips), the entrance to the vagina, and the clitoris.

W

warheads (wawr´ hĕdz´) slang. offensive. Large breasts that are revealed in a tight sweater.

wash room noun. euphemism. The toilet.

* **water (to pass)** verb phrase. euphemism. Urinate.

water the lilies (... lĭ lēz) verb phrase. male slang. Urinate.

water one's pony verb phrase. slang. Urinate.

* **watermelons** noun, plural. slang. A woman's breasts.

* **water sports** noun, plural. slang. Urinating on one's partner during sexual play.

waxing the cucumber verb phrase. slang. Masturbation.

wee wee (wē wē) 1. verb. children's word. Urinate. 2. noun. children's word. Urine.

* **well-endowed** (wĕl ĕn dowd) adjective. slang. 1. (For a male) having a large penis. 2. (For a female) having large breasts.

---

* **wet**   1. verb. euphemism.   Urinate.   "The baby *wet* his pants."
2. adjective. slang.   A sexually aroused woman gets *wet*. That
is, her vagina becomes well lubricated.

wet-dreams   (wĕt drēmz)   noun. euphemism.   A dream
of sexual contact that results in ejaculation of semen during
sleep.   A nocturnal emission.

whack off   (wăk awf)   verb. vulgar.   Masturbate.

whang   (wăng)   noun. vulgar.   The penis.

* **whore**   (hor)   noun. vulgar.   A prostitute.   A woman who
charges money for an act of sexual intercourse.

* **wick**   (wĭk)   noun. slang.   The penis.   (A wick is the
string in a candle) to *dip one's wick* is to have sexual
intercourse.

* **wiener**   (wē nur)   noun. slang, children's word.   The
penis.   (Wiener is another word for hot dog.)

wife-swapping   (wīf swŏp´ ĭng)   noun.   Exchange of
wives for an evening in order to create new sexual excitement.

* **withdrawal**   (wĭth draw´ ŭl)   noun. general use.   A
method of birth control, not very effective.   During intercourse,
at the moment of ejaculation, the man withdraws his penis
from the vagina and ejaculates outside his partner in order to
prevent pregnancy.

womb   (wūm)   noun. general use.   The uterus.

woody   (wŭ´ dē)   noun. slang.   An erection.

* **working girl**   noun. slang.   A prostitute.

X

X.Y.Z.   Examine Your Zipper!   (Your fly is open.)   A "secret"
code among boys and men to discreetly let another know that
he should zipper up his pants.

X-rated   (ĕks´ ra´ tĭd)   adjective. general use.   For mature
adults only.   A movie considered to be pornographic and
unsuitable for young audiences.   When a movie is rated "X,"
only persons over the age of 18 may enter the theater.

y

yank off (yănk awf)　verb. vulgar.　Masturbate.

you know what you can do with it!　exclamation. slang.
Euphemism for "shove it up your ass."　(I don't want it.)

your you-know-what　noun. euphemism.　1. Sex organ
(usually penis). 2. Anus.　"Shove it up your *you-know-what!*"

"Don't you ever touch my little Dick again!"

Bibliography

Alford, Richard D. and William J. O'Donnell — "Linguistic Scale: Cussing and Euphemisms" *Maledicta* Vol 7, p. 155–163, 1983.

Aman, Reinhold, Editor — *Maledicta: The International Journal of Verbal Aggression* Maledicta Press, Vol 4–8, Waukesha, Wisconsin, 1980–1985.

— "Offensive Language Via Computer" Op. cit. Vol 8, p. 105.

— "Offensive Words in Dictionaries" Op. cit. Vol 8, p. 123–153.

— "Words Can Kill: The Anatomy of a Murder" Op. cit. Vol 8, p. 5.

Ashley, Leonard R. N. — "Dyke Diction: The Language of Lesbians" *Maledicta* Vol 6, p. 123, 1982.

Boston Women's Health Collective — *Our Bodies, Our Selves* Simon and Schuster, New York, 1976.

Clifton, Merrill — "How to Hate Thy Neighbor: A Guide to Racist Maledicta" *Maledicta* Vol 2, p. 149–173, 1978.

Fine, Gary Allen — "Rude Words: Insults and Narration in Preadolescent Obscene Talk" *Maledicta* Vol 5, p. 51–68, 1981.

French, Lawrence — "Racial and Ethnic Slurs: Regional Awareness and Variations" *Maledicta* Vol 4, p. 117, 1980.

Hentoff, Nat — "The Deflowering of the American Heritage Dictionary" *The Village Voice* Oct. 11, 1983, p.6 reprinted in *Maledicta* Vol 7, p. 121–128, 1983.

Morris, William, editor — *The American Heritage Dictionary of the English Language.* Houghton Mifflin Company, Boston, 1976.

Preston, Dennis R. — "Lusty Language Learning: Confessions on Acquiring Polish" *Maledicta* Vol 6, p. 117–120, 1982.

Spears, Richard A. — *"Slang and Euphemism: A Dictionary of Oaths, Curses, Insults, Sexual Slang and Metaphor, Racial Slurs, Drug Talk, Homosexual Lingo and Related Matters.* New American Library, New York, 1981.

Terry, Roger L. — "A Connotative Analysis of Synonyms for Sexual Intercourse" *Maledicta* Vol 7, p. 237–252, 1983.

Wentworth, Harold and Stuart Berg Flexner, compilers and editors— *Dictionary of American Slang*, second supplemented edition, Thomas Crowell Company, New York, 1975.

Wilson, Wayne J. — "Five Years and 121 Dirty Words Later" *Maledicta* Vol 5, p. 243–254, 1981.